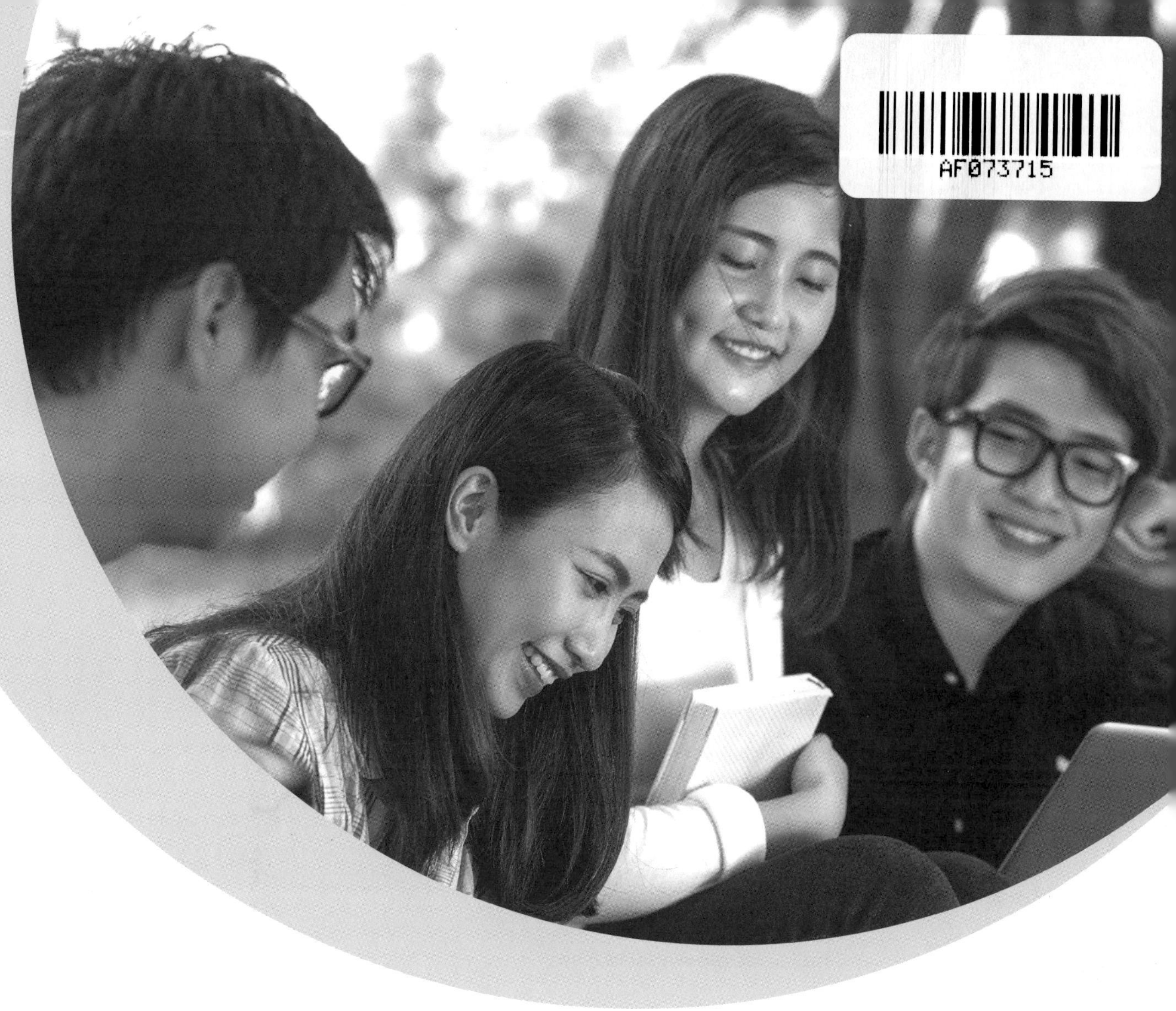

GCSE Chinese
Practice Workbook and Papers

Kou You, Haiyan Yin, Yadi Luo

Cypress Books

GCSE Chinese Practice Workbook and Papers

Kou You, Haiyan Yin, Yadi Luo

Editor: Xue Mei
Commissioning editor: Chengqian Guo
English proofreader: Suzanne Cummings
Cover design: Beijing Wutongying Computer Technology Co., Ltd
Layout design: Beijing Wutongying Computer Technology Co., Ltd

First published in Great Britain in 2022 by Cypress Book Co. (U.K.) Ltd.
Unit 6, Provident Industrial Estate
Pump Lane, Hayes
London UB3 3NE
United Kingdom
Tel: 0044 (0)20 88481500
E-mail: info@cypressbooks.com

Find us at www.cypressbooks.com

Text copyright © 2022 by Kou You, Haiyan Yin, Yadi Luo
The moral rights of the authors have been asserted.

All rights reserved. No part of this publication may be reproduced or transmitted by any means, electronic, mechanical, photocopying or otherwise, without the prior permission of the publisher.

ISBN: 978-1-84570-045-4

2nd printing in China 2024

About the Authors

Kou You graduated with a Master's Degree from the Institute of Education, University of London. She was trained in the UK and works as a Mandarin teacher. She has over 10 years teaching experience and she still enjoys the daily teaching practice. She shares her teaching experience at different training sessions and she brings what she has learned back into her teaching.

After graduating with a BA English Degree from Jishou University, Haiyan Yin furthered her study and attained a Master's Degree in Translation from London Metropolitan University. Haiyan started teaching Mandarin in secondary schools in 2008 and has since accumulated 14 years' experience in teaching GCSE and A Level courses. Haiyan set up and led the Mandarin department in the UCL Academy from 2012 to 2020, during which time the UCL Academy became the biggest GCSE exam centre in the UK. Haiyan also initiated and ran the Confucius Classroom and MEP programme at the UCL Academy, as well as becoming a PGCE mentor and working as an examiner for various British exam boards. Currently, Haiyan is working at St Dominic International School, teaching IB language A.

Yadi Luo has been teaching Mandarin for nearly 20 years. She is currently working as the head of Mandarin and Confucius Classroom manager in a north London secondary school, one of the first MEP schools when the programme was launched in 2016. She was awarded the title "Excellent Mandarin Teacher" by IOE in 2017 and became a GCSE examiner in 2019. As an experienced classroom practitioner, Yadi is often invited to deliver workshops or keynote speeches by UCL. Yadi's students have won awards in many Mandarin competitions including the success in securing a scholarship from the "Chinese Bridge" competition in 2021.

作者简介

寇优，伦敦大学教育学院教育学硕士。现为英国主流学校QTS持牌教师，同时任教于英国中小学，并担任英国教师资格培训导师，曾获评2013年度优秀教师。2011—2020年多次担任汉办英国孔子学院考试局中文考官，英国中小学生中文活动比赛评委，北爱尔兰、威尔士及苏格兰地区中文教学技能大赛评委。著有《英国小学汉语言教育资源库—教师手册》一书。

尹海燕，本科毕业于吉首大学英语教育专业，硕士毕业于英国伦敦都市大学应用翻译专业。在伦敦从事中学中文教学已有十四年，曾担任伦敦大学附属中学中文部主管和英国教师资格培训导师。具有十二年的GCSE和A level课程教学经验，同时担任A level和GCSE考试阅卷官，具有丰富的试题编写经验。目前在圣多米尼克国际学校教授IB中文课程。

罗雅荻，从事国际中文教学近二十年。现任伦敦北部中学中文部及孔子课堂主管，英国中文培优项目资深教师，多次受邀担任UCL中文教学工作坊及中文大会主题发言人，2017年荣获IOE年度优秀中文教师，还曾参与2019年度GCSE中考判卷。其历年所教学生多次获得地区或国家级中文比赛奖项，包括2021年"汉语桥"世界大中小学生中文比赛。

How to Use This Book?

This book is designed for students who need to prepare for the General Certificate of Secondary Education (GCSE) Chinese exam and teachers who need to tutor GCSE candidates. The book consists of 12 chapters, the first 9 of which each cover a GCSE related topic, covering all topics in the two new syllabuses of the GCSE exam. Chapter 10 is a classic reading exercise, Chapter 11 is a listening practice paper, and Chapter 12 is a reading practice paper. Based on the frequency of GCSE topics in students' lives and exams, there are more practice questions for the most frequent topics, so the number of questions varies from chapter to chapter. Through these exercises, students will be able to study and master key GCSE topics with a clearer aim.

The first 9 chapters of this book each contain four sections: Listening, Speaking, Reading and Writing. The skill-oriented exercises can help students improve their Chinese proficiency and get them ready for the GCSE exam. The 9 chapters do not have a fixed teaching order, so teachers and students can use them accordingly. The practice papers in Chapters 11 and 12 can be used in class, as homework, as group exercises, or as an individual test. In addition, all questions are marked with points for teachers to evaluate students or students to evaluate themselves.

In addition to the text of the 12 chapters, the book also provides the listening transcript and the answer key to the practice questions. The listening transcript is in the appendix of the book, and the answer key can be obtained by scanning the QR code on the back cover. Students can scan the QR code on the back cover to listen to the recording. After completing the questions, students can refer to the listening transcript in the appendix. The examiner version and the examinee version of the speaking practice questions are provided in the Speaking section. Teachers use the examiner version, and students use the examinee version. The reading exercises cover all reading questions in the new GCSE exam, including Chinese-English translation, English-Chinese translation and poetry reading exercises. The writing section also covers all types of the writing questions in the new GCSE exam, including picture-based writing, short essay, long essay and English-Chinese translation, etc. In addition, some of the questions in the book are marked with "Challenge". Those are relatively difficult exercises for students to selectively perfect their practice based on their Chinese level.

Wish all the GCSE Chinese candidates the best of luck in your exam!

如何使用这本书？

本书专为需要准备GCSE（General Certificate of Secondary Education）中文考试的学生和需要辅导GCSE考生的老师设计。全书共包含12个章节，前9个章节每章均涉及一个GCSE相关话题，全书涵盖GCSE两种新考试大纲中的所有话题。第10章为经典文本阅读练习，第11章为听力模拟题，第12章为阅读模拟题。基于GCSE各话题在学生生活中和考试中出现的频率不同，本书针对高频话题设置了更多练习题目，因此不同章节的题目数量并不一样。通过这些练习，学生将能更有针对性地学习和掌握GCSE重点话题。

本书前9个章节每章均包含听力、口语、阅读和写作四大板块，针对听、说、读、写四项语言技能设置练习题，可帮助学生全面提高中文水平，为中文中考做好准备。9个章节之间并无固定的先后顺序，老师和学生可根据自身情况按照任意顺序使用。第11、12章的模拟题既可以在上课时使用，也可以作为学生作业，既可以用作小组练习，也可以由单个学生独立完成。此外，所有题目均标注分值，便于老师评估学生及学生自我评估。

除12章正文内容以外，本书还提供录音文本和练习题答案，录音文本位于本书附录，练习题答案则需扫描封底二维码获取。在完成听力练习时，学生可以扫描本书封底二维码获取录音，完成题目后，可查看附录中的录音文本。口语练习提供考官版本和考生版本的题目，老师使用考官版本，学生使用考生版本，使用时需注意区分。阅读练习涵盖新版GCSE考试所有阅读题型，包括汉译英、英译汉和诗歌阅读练习等。写作部分也涵盖了新版GCSE考试所有写作题型，包括看图写作文、小作文、大作文及英译汉练习等。此外，书中部分标注"Challenge"的题目属于难度较高的练习题，供学生根据自己中文水平有选择地进行拓展练习。

最后，预祝所有考生都能取得好成绩！

目录 | CONTENTS

I. Me, My Family and My Friends
- Listening 1
- Speaking 5
- Reading 10
- Writing 15

II. Free Time Activities
- Listening 20
- Speaking 24
- Reading 33
- Writing 39

III. Technology in Everyday Life
- Listening 43
- Speaking 45
- Reading 50
- Writing 52

IV. Customs and Festivals
- Listening 56
- Speaking 57
- Reading 60
- Writing 62

V. Where You Live
- Listening 66
- Speaking 71
- Reading 90
- Writing 100

VI. Travel and Tourism
- Listening 107

   Speaking *113*
   Reading *122*
   Writing *129*

VII. Lifestyle
   Listening *134*
   Speaking *136*
   Reading *143*
   Writing *145*

VIII. Social and Global Issues
   Listening *148*
   Speaking *149*
   Reading *157*
   Writing *160*

IX. Education, Future Study and Employment
   Listening *163*
   Speaking *167*
   Reading *171*
   Writing *175*

X. Old Sayings, Poems and Classic Passages
   Mencius *177*
   Poems *178*

XI. Listening Practice Papers
   Paper I *182*
   Paper II *191*
   Paper III *200*

XII. Reading Practice Papers
   Paper I *209*
   Paper II *221*
   Paper III *233*

Transcript *244*

Me, My Family and My Friends

 Listening

❖ Family and Personalities ❖

1. These primary pupils are talking about their family members. What do they say about them? Listen to the recordings and give one detail in **English** for each question.

   Example: What does this pupil's dad look like?
   _____Tall and handsome_____

   (1) How does this pupil describe her mum's appearance? (1 mark)

   (2) How does this pupil describe his relationship with his elder sister? (1 mark)

   (3) What does this pupil think of her younger brother? (1 mark)

I. Me, My Family and My Friends

✧ My Family ✧

2. Listen to the whole paragraph and choose a correct option to complete each statement. Write the letters in the blanks.

Example: My dad is _____C_____ .

A	a doctor
B	a chef
C	an engineer
D	a teacher

(1) My mum _____ . (1 mark)

A	is not busy
B	is a housewife
C	has lots of work
D	loves shopping

(2) My elder sister _____ . (1 mark)

A	walks to school
B	is Chinese
C	loves reading
D	is two years older than me

(3) My elder sister _____ . (1 mark)

A	is a secondary student
B	likes cooking
C	is a university student
D	is 14 years old

✧ Describing People and Personalities ✧

3. Listen to the whole paragraph and choose one correct statement for each person. Write the letters in the blanks.

   Ma Li (马丽) _____   **Xiaotian** (小田) _____   **Daming** (大明) _____

A	I am a bit chubby.
B	I am Australian.
C	I like outdoor activities.
D	I am very kind.
E	I would like to be an actor.
F	I can speak Spanish.
G	I like to play football.

✧ Marriage and Relationships ✧

4. Two friends are chatting about their views and plans on marriage and relationships. Answer the questions in **English.**

   Person 1
   Example: What did **she** want for her marriage in the past?
   _____A big wedding_____

   (1) How does she feel about it now? (1 mark)

   (2) What does she **NOT** want in the future? (1 mark)

   Person 2

   (3) What was **his** view on this topic when he was little? (1 mark)

I. Me, My Family and My Friends

(4) What is his marital status now? (1 mark)

(5) What is his family plan for the future? (1 mark)

✦ Mr Wang and His Family ✦

5. Listen to the recording and choose a word/phrase from the box to complete each sentence below. You need to write the words/phrases in the blanks. There are more words/phrases than blanks.

last December	skiing	singing	last November
very good	three	spring	five
very bad	~~four~~	dancing	

Example: There are ____four____ people in Mr Wang's family.

(1) Mr Wang's daughter likes _____. (1 mark)

(2) The Wang family's relationship is _____. (1 mark)

(3) _____, they went skiing together. (1 mark)

 **Speaking**

◆ Situation-based test

Topic: My new friend `Challenge`

For teachers

» The teacher will start the conversation by greeting and introducing his/her role.
» The teacher can only read out the questions listed below in order and the questions cannot be repeated more than twice.

You are asking your brother about a new friend he made during his China trip.

1	你的朋友多大了？ Allow the candidate to answer.
2	他/她喜欢做什么运动？ Allow the candidate to answer.
3	你们在中国一起参加了什么活动？ Allow the candidate to answer.
4	☺! surprising question 你在中国待了多长时间？ Allow the candidate to answer.
5	☺? a question Allow the candidate to ask if you want to visit China in the future. *Answer briefly.*

I. Me, My Family and My Friends

Topic: My new friend

For candidates

You are asking your brother about a new friend he made during his China trip.

» Your teacher will start the conversation by greeting you and introducing his/her role.

» You will answer the following five questions in order.

» The question ☺! is an unprepared question.

» The question ☺? is a question you need to ask your teacher.

1. Say how old your friend is.
2. Say what sports your friend likes to do.
3. Say what activities you took part in together when in China.
4. ☺!
5. ☺?
   Ask if your sister wants to visit China in the future.

◆ **Picture-based test**

Topic: My free time Challenge

For teachers

» The speaking task should last **two-and-a-half to three minutes**.
» The teacher should ask the exact questions listed below in order, and cannot repeat the questions more than twice.
» The teacher can ask follow-up questions using "还有呢？" and "为什么？" to prompt extended answers.

1. 描述这张照片。（还有呢？）
2. 你觉得去公园好不好？（为什么？还有呢？）
3. 上个星期，你在公园做了什么？（还有呢？）
4. 你和家人在一起的时候，你们会做什么？（还有呢？）
5. 今年暑假，你想做什么？（还有呢？）

I. Me, My Family and My Friends

Topic: My free time

For candidates

» Write all your notes on a separate A4 paper.
» Answer the following questions in order.
» You can ask your teacher to repeat questions.

Look at the photo and prepare to answer the following questions in order:

1. Describe the photo;
2. Your opinion of going to parks;
3. What you did in the park last week;
4. What things you normally do with your family;
5. What you would like to do this summer holiday.

💬 Two-way discussion questions

All about me

1. _{Nǐ xìng shénme? Jiào shénme? Duō dà le? Shàng jǐ niánjí?}
   你姓什么？叫什么？多大了？上几年级？ (4 marks)

2. _{Nǐ jiā yǒu jǐ kǒu rén?}
   你家有几口人？ (1 mark)

3. _{Nǐ juéde nǐ de jiārén zěnmeyàng? Nǐ zuì xǐhuan shéi?}
   你觉得你的家人怎么样？你最喜欢谁？ (2 marks)

4. _{Nǐ zhōumò tōngcháng hé jiārén yìqǐ zuò shénme?}
   你周末通常和家人一起做什么？ (1 mark)

5. _{Shéi shì nǐ zuì hǎo de péngyou? Wèi shénme xǐhuan tā/tā?}
   谁是你最好的朋友？为什么喜欢他/她？ (2 marks)

6. _{Nǐ yǒu nán/nǚ péngyou ma?}
   你有男/女朋友吗？ (1 mark)

7. _{Nǐ juéde zhōngxuéshēng tán liàn'ài yǒu shénme hǎochù hé huàichù?}
   你觉得中学生谈恋爱有什么好处和坏处？ (5 marks)

I. Me, My Family and My Friends

Lili's Family Challenge

1. **Lili** (黎黎) is given Mandarin writing homework about her family and the following are the extracts from her essay. Read it and choose the correct statements for each question. Write the letters in the blanks.

> ……
> 最近我和妈妈在一起不太开心，因为我除了要做学校的作业以外，还要做她给我的作业。我的卧室很干净，但是她总是让我多打扫。我压力这么大，哪儿有时间啊？
> 我爸爸长得矮矮胖胖的，特别可爱。他的能力也特别强：工作的时候，他会帮助生病的人；在家的时候，他会做饭，会整理花园，还会给我和妈妈做漂亮的裙子。

(1) Why is **Lili** not so happy with her mum right now? Choose two reasons. _____ (2 marks)

A	Mum is in a bad mood recently.
B	Mum thinks that she makes too many mistakes in her homework.
C	Mum gives her extra homework.
D	Mum sends her to her bedroom too often.
E	Mum doesn't think her bedroom is clean enough.

(2) Which **three** statements are mentioned about **Lili**'s dad in the text? _____ (3 marks)

A	He is tall and handsome.
B	He is short and chubby.
C	According to Lili, he could be a designer or an engineer.
D	According to Lili, he could be a doctor or a nurse.
E	He is incredibly capable at home.
F	He is not a handyman at home.

Daming and Xiaomei Challenge

2. Read the passage below and choose the right answers for the sentences. Write the letters in the blanks.

> 大明（Daming）在一个公司工作，他的工作很忙。大明的女朋友叫小美（Xiaomei），小美是一个兼职护士。
>
> 每个星期日，他们都一起去超市买食物。有时候，他们也一起去购物中心买衣服。他们还喜欢一起去电影院看电影。
>
> 大明和小美希望明年结婚。结婚以后，他们想去中国工作，因为中国有很多工作机会。

Example: Daming works in a _____D_____.

A	Help Centre
B	school
C	hospital
D	company

(1) **Xiaomei** is a _____. (1 mark)

A	full time doctor
B	part-time nurse
C	part-time doctor
D	full time nurse

(2) What is **NOT** mentioned that **Daming** and **Xiaomei** do together? _____ (1 mark)

A	Going to gym
B	Food shopping
C	Clothes shopping
D	Going to the cinema

I. Me, My Family and My Friends

(3) When will **Daming** and **Xiaomei** get married? _____ (1 mark)

A	Next June
B	This Christmas
C	This Year
D	Next year

(4) Where would **Daming** and **Xiaomei** like to work after they get married?

_____ (1 mark)

A	Spain
B	Singapore
C	China
D	Canada

(5) Why do **Daming** and **Xiaomei** want to move to another country after married?

_____ (1 mark)

A	Lots of job opportunities
B	Very easy jobs
C	Earn lots of money
D	Work four days per week

❖ Me and My Friend ❖

3. Read the passage below and choose the right answer for each question.

> 我是一个中学生，今年十五岁。我每个星期六下午都去游泳。我觉得游泳很健康，也很有趣。我有很多爱好，除了游泳以外，我还喜欢踢足球。我和我的同学一起踢足球。
>
> 我的弟弟叫小明（Xiaoming）。他个子很高，喜欢打篮球，也喜欢玩电脑游戏。每个星期日，他都会玩一个小时的电脑游戏。

我的好朋友叫小丽（Xiaoli）。她是我的同学，她很瘦，是法国人。我们每天一起吃午饭、一起做作业。有时候，我们也喜欢一起买东西。

Example: Who has lots of hobbies? _____A_____

A	The author
B	The author's elder brother
C	The author's younger brother
D	Xiaoli

(1) How does the author describe her younger brother? _____ (1 mark)

A	Very kind
B	Very funny
C	Very tall
D	Very slim

(2) What does the author's younger brother do every Sunday? _____ (1 mark)

A	Go shopping
B	Play basketball
C	Go swimming
D	Play computer games

(3) What does the author **NOT** do with **Xiaoli**? _____ (1 mark)

A	Play football
B	Have lunch
C	Do homework
D	Go shopping

My Grandparents

4. Read the passage below and answer the questions in **English**.

> 我的爷爷是中国人，他住在中国北京。我的爷爷很高，也很帅，他的头发很短。他去过很多国家，他去过英国、法国和德国，等等。他会说英语。
>
> 我的奶奶是法国人。她年轻的时候很喜欢运动，她以前是网球运动员。她很高，也很瘦。
>
> 我的爸爸跟我的爷爷奶奶一样，很高，但是他不喜欢运动，他喜欢看电影。我爸爸是一个工程师，他喜欢他的工作。

(1) Who can speak English? (1 mark)

(2) What does the author's grandma look like? (1 mark)

(3) What is the hobby of the author's dad? (1 mark)

(4) What does the author's dad think about his job? (1 mark)

 **Writing**

1. Write an article based on the photo below. You **must** mention the following points:
   » describe the photo;
   » give your opinion on your friends.
   Write approximately **30-40 Chinese characters**. (12 marks)

2. You have a pen pal in China. Write an e-mail to your pen pal to introduce you and your little brother. You **must** include the following information:
   » what your little brother likes to do;
   » what activities you and your little brother do together;
   » when you and your little brother do the activities;

I. Me, My Family and My Friends

» how the relationship is between you and your little brother.

Write approximately **50-60 Chinese characters**. (16 marks)

3. Write an article to describe one of your friends. You need to mention the following points:
   » your friend's name and how old your friend is;
   » what kind of person your friend is;
   » what activity you did with your friend last week;
   » what is your friend's plan for the future.

   Write approximately **90-120 Chinese characters**. (20 marks)

4. You are invited to write an article for your local newspaper to express your opinion on whether social media is helping people establish relationships. You **must** mention the following points:
   » your experience of using social media;
   » your opinion whether the social media is helping people establish relationships and the reasons;
   » advantages and disadvantages of using social media to establish relationships;
   » how could social media do more to help establish relationships.

   To score high, you need to give opinions and justifications using high level vocabulary and complex sentence structures.

   Write approximately **150-200 Chinese characters**. (Challenge) (28 marks)

I. Me, My Family and My Friends

5. Translate these sentences into **Chinese**.

   (1) I live in Beijing. (2 marks)

   (2) She has two younger brothers. (2 marks)

   (3) He does sports at 10 o'clock. (2 marks)

   (4) My friend is both tall and thin. (3 marks)

   (5) Last Saturday, I played football with my friend. (3 marks)

6. Translate the paragraph into **Chinese**. Challenge

> I am in Year 11. I like doing sports and learning languages. On Monday, I have a Mandarin lesson. I want to work in China as an English teacher in the future, because being an English teacher in China is very cool.
>
> (12 marks)

_____

_____

_____

_____

_____

_____

I. Me, My Family and My Friends

11 Free Time Activities

 Listening

❖ Food ❖

1. **Xiaoying** (小英), **Xiaomei** (小美) and **Ma Tian** (马田) are talking about food. Listen to the conversation and complete the statements by choosing the correct options. Write the letters in the blanks.

    (1) **Xiaoying** likes to eat _____ and chicken. (1 mark)

A	fish
B	tomato
C	vegetable
D	rice

    (2) **Xiaomei** likes to eat _____. (1 mark)

A	fast food
B	healthy food
C	fried rice
D	chicken

    (3) **Ma Tian** likes to eat _____. (1 mark)

A	Chinese food
B	Spanish food
C	French food
D	Japanese food

20   GCSE Chinese Practice Workbook and Papers

✈ Sports Challenge ✦

2. **Xiaoshan** (小山) is talking about sports. Listen to the whole paragraph and choose **three** correct statements. Write the letters in the boxes. ☐ ☐ ☐   (3 marks)

A	Every Monday, **Xiaoshan** swims with his friend.
B	**Xiaoshan** swims for half an hour every time.
C	**Xiaoshan** swims better than his little brother.
D	**Xiaoshan**'s little brother can't play basketball.
E	**Xiaoshan** and his dad both like playing tennis.
F	**Xiaoshan**'s dad does sport every Thursday.
G	**Xiaoshan**'s mum likes running.

✈ Music ✦

3. **Dalin** (大林) and **Xiaomei** (小美) are talking about music. Listen to the conversation and choose the correct answer for each question. Write the letters in the blanks.

(1) What will **Xiaomei** do on Saturday? _____   (1 mark)

A	Watch TV
B	Go to a concert
C	Go to a zoo
D	Dance

(2) What will **Dalin** do on Sunday? _____   (1 mark)

A	Perform singing
B	Perform dancing
C	Go to a music festival
D	See a film

(3) When is the Chinese music festival? _____ (1 mark)

A	This month
B	This Saturday
C	Next Sunday
D	Next month

❖ Eating Out Challenge ❖

4. **Fangfang** (方方) is travelling in Beijing. She is interviewed by a journalist in a Chinese restaurant. Listen to the conversation and answer the questions in **English**.

   (1) What food will **Fangfang** eat today? (1 mark)

   (2) Apart from egg fried rice and lamb, what else did **Fangfang** eat in Beijing? (1 mark)

   (3) What flavour is **Fangfang**'s favourite? (1 mark)

   (4) What food does **Fangfang** want to eat? (1 mark)

   (5) Why can **Fangfang** only eat fast food tomorrow morning? (1 mark)

❖ TV Challenge ❖

5. Two friends are chatting about TV programmes. Listen to their individual description and answer the questions in **English**.

   Friend 1

   Example: What did **she** like watching when **she** was little?

Animation

(1) What programmes does **she** like watching now? (1 mark)

(2) What programmes does **she** want to watch more in the future? (1 mark)

Friend 2

(3) What did **he** like watching before? (1 mark)

(4) What programmes does **he** often watch now? (1 mark)

(5) What programmes does **he** plan to watch more in the future? (1 mark)

·❥ Celebrities Challenge ❥·

6. A group of film directors are talking about the current film industry.
   Write **L** if the director **likes** the mentioned perspective of the festival,
       D if the director **dislikes** the mentioned perspective of the festival,
   or **M** if the opinion is **mixed**.

   (1) ☐ (1 mark)
   (2) ☐ (1 mark)
   (3) ☐ (1 mark)
   (4) ☐ (1 mark)

 **Speaking**

◆ **Situation-based test 1**

Topic: Sports

For teachers

» The teacher will start the conversation by greeting and introducing his/her role.
» The teacher can only read out the questions listed below in order and the questions cannot be repeated more than twice.

You are talking to a friend about sports.

1	你喜欢什么运动？ Allow the candidate to answer.
2	你一般星期几运动？ Allow the candidate to answer.
3	你觉得做运动对我们有什么好处？ Allow the candidate to answer.
4	☺! surprising question 你常常和谁一起运动？ Allow the candidate to answer.
5	☺? a question Allow the candidate to ask where you often go to do sports. *Answer briefly.*

Topic: Sports

For candidates

You are talking to a friend about sports.

» Your teacher will start the conversation by greeting you and introducing his/her role.

» You will answer the following five questions in order.

» The question ☺! is an unprepared question.

» The question ☺? is a question you need to ask your teacher.

---

1. Say what sports you like.
2. Say which day of the week you normally do sports.
3. Say how sports can benefit us.
4. ☺!
5. ☺?
   Ask where your friend often goes to do sports.

II. Free Time Activities

◆ **Situation-based test 2**

Topic: Food `Challenge`

For teachers

» The teacher will start the conversation by greeting and introducing his/her role.
» The teacher can only read out the questions listed below in order and the questions cannot be repeated more than twice.

You are talking to your friend about food.

1	你最喜欢吃什么？ Allow the candidate to answer.
2	你觉得什么是健康饮食？ Allow the candidate to answer.
3	☺! surprising question 你吃过什么中国菜？ Allow the candidate to answer.
4	☺? a question Allow the candidate to ask what you ate for dinner last night. *Answer briefly.*
5	☺? a question Allow the candidate to ask what you would like to eat tomorrow. *Answer briefly.*

Topic: Food `Challenge`

For candidates

You are talking to your friend about food.

» Your teacher will start the conversation by greeting you and introducing his/her role.

» You will answer the following five questions in order.

» The question ☺! is an unprepared question.

» The question ☺? is a question you need to ask your teacher.

---

1. Say what your favourite food is.
2. Say what you think is a healthy diet.
3. ☺!
4. ☺?
   Ask what your friend ate for dinner last night.
5. ☺?
   Ask what your friend would like to eat tomorrow.

II. Free Time Activities

◆ **Picture-based test 1**

Topic: Eating out

For teachers

» The speaking task should last **two-and-a-half to three minutes**.
» The teacher should ask the exact questions listed below in order, and cannot repeat the questions more than twice.
» The teacher can ask follow-up questions using "还有呢？" and "为什么？" to prompt extended answers.

1. 描述这张照片。（还有呢？）
2. 你觉得出去吃饭好不好？（为什么？还有呢？）
3. 你上次去饭店吃了什么？（还有呢？）
4. 你会做什么菜？（还有呢？）
5. 你想学做什么菜？（为什么？还有呢？）

Topic: Eating out

For candidates

» Write all your notes on a separate A4 paper.
» Answer the following questions in order.
» You can ask your teacher to repeat questions.

Look at the photo and prepare to answer the following questions in order:

1. Describe the photo;
2. Your opinion on eating out;
3. What you ate the last time when you went to a restaurant;
4. What food you can make;
5. What dish you would like to learn to cook.

◆ **Picture-based test 2**

Topic: Doing Sports Challenge

For teachers

» The speaking task should last **three to three-and-a-half minutes**.
» The teacher should ask the exact questions listed below in order, and cannot repeat the questions more than twice.
» The teacher can ask follow up questions using "还有呢？"and"为什么？"to prompt extended answers.

1. 描述这张照片。（还有呢？）
2. 你觉得运动好不好？（为什么？还有呢？）
3. 你上次运动是什么时候？（还有呢？）
4. 你每次运动多长时间？（还有呢？）
5. 你这个周末想做什么运动？（还有呢？）

Topic: Doing Sports

For candidates

» Write all your notes on a separate A4 paper.
» Answer the following questions in order.
» You can ask your teacher to repeat questions.
» ☺! means you will answer an unprepared question.

Look at the photo and prepare to answer the following questions in order:

1. Describe the photo;
2. Your opinion on doing sports;
3. When was the last time you did sports;
4. How long you spend doing sports each time;
5. ☺!

II. Free Time Activities

Two-way discussion questions

Hobbies and spare time

1. 你有什么爱好? (1 mark)

2. 你喜欢听什么音乐？为什么？ (2 marks)

3. 你更喜欢看电影还是看电视？为什么？ (2 marks)

4. 你喜欢做运动吗？你喜欢做什么运动？ (2 marks)

5. 你上次去健身房是什么时候？你觉得怎么样？ (3 marks)

 Reading

Food Challenge

1. Read these notes from **Xiaoshan** (小山), **Lingling** (玲玲) and **Daming** (大明). Choose a word/phrase from the box below to complete each sentence. There are more words/phrases than blanks.

小山：每星期五，我和我的家人都去中国饭店吃饭，因为我和我的家人都喜欢吃中国菜。我家前面有一个非常好的中国饭店，也很干净。

玲玲：我喜欢做饭，我的哥哥和姐姐也都喜欢做饭。每天，我和我的家人一起做饭，我们做米饭、肉和青菜。我觉得在家做饭很健康。晚饭以后，我和我的哥哥姐姐做作业，我的爸爸一边看电视一边喝茶，我的妈妈看书。

大明：我的家人有时候在晚上买外卖，因为我的爸爸妈妈工作很忙，他们没有时间做饭。我觉得买外卖非常方便。我们也喜欢用信用卡。

running	chicken	Japanese	sports
credit card	Chinese	takeaway	Spanish
cooking	reading	pizza	cash
drinks tea			

(1) **Xiaoshan** and his family go to a _____ restaurant every Friday. (1 mark)

(2) **Lingling** likes _____ and so do her elder sister and elder brother. (1 mark)

(3) After dinner, **Lingling**'s dad _____ whilst watching TV. (1 mark)

(4) **Daming** and his family sometimes have _____ for their dinner. (1 mark)

(5) **Daming** pays for dinner with a _____ . (1 mark)

⇥ Sports Centre ⇤

2. This sports centre advertisement below is on a community website. Write your answers in **English** in the blanks to complete each statement.

> 健康运动中心
>
> - 我们在市中心，旁边有火车站，可以免费停车，非常方便。
> - 大人每月300元，小孩每月150元。
> - 运动中心每周开门七天。早上六点开门，晚上十点半关门。
> - 运动中心有网球场、足球场、游泳池和跑步机。
> - 如果你累了，也可以去我们的咖啡店。

(1) The sports centre is in the _____ . (1 mark)

(2) The sports centre has a free _____ . (1 mark)

(3) In the morning, the sports centre opens at _____ . (1 mark)

(4) The sports centre has tennis courts, a football pitch, a _____ and running machines. (1 mark)

(5) If you need a rest, you can go to the _____ in this sports centre. (1 mark)

⇥ Music Challenge ⇤

3. **Han Li** (韩丽) and **Pan Hao** (潘浩) are talking about their opinions on music.

> 韩丽：
>
> 　　我年轻的时候特别喜欢听英国摇滚乐，越吵越好，因为它能让我很兴奋。但是现在生活里有很多不开心的事，我更喜欢听能让我平静的音乐。总的来说，我不知道如果没有音乐，人类的生活会变成什么样。

潘浩：

我一直很喜欢古典音乐，它能让我特别放松。最近，我还爱上了流行音乐，因为它很受年轻人欢迎，我希望能跟我的女儿有更多聊天儿的机会。对我来说，音乐是老天给人类最好的礼物。

Who do the following statements apply to?

Tick **H** if the statement applies to **Han Li**,

　P if the statement applies to **Pan Hao**,

　or both boxes if the statement applies to both **Han Li** and **Pan Hao**.

(1) I've always been a fan of classical music. (1 mark)

　H ☐　　P ☐

(2) I loved very loud music. (1 mark)

　H ☐　　P ☐

(3) I like music that calms me down. (1 mark)

　H ☐　　P ☐

(4) I think that music is the best thing in one's life. (1 mark)

　H ☐　　P ☐

(5) I hope to be able to talk to my daughter more often through pop music. (1 mark)

　H ☐　　P ☐

❖ Cinema and TV　Challenge ❖

4. Read the survey below on people's preferences on cinema and TV. Answer the questions in **English**.

一家电影公司访问了住在英国的南方人、北方人和中部人。
- 北方人：喜欢在电视上看老电影，因为更便宜。
- 中部人：更喜欢去电影院看电影，因为能看到最新的电影。
- 南方人：有的喜欢在家看电影，有的喜欢去电影院。在家看时可以和家人一边看，一边聊天儿。在电影院，电影的音效更好，而且还有很多美味的零食。

II. Free Time Activities

(1) Why do the **northerners** prefer to watch films on TV? (1 mark)

(2) Why do the **central people** like going to cinema? (1 mark)

(3) Why do **some southerners** like watching films at home? (1 mark)

(4) Name **two** reasons why **some southerners** prefer cinemas? (2 marks)
   ①
   ②

·✧ Celebrity Challenge ✧·

5. **Wu Yue** (伍月) is talking about her idol. Answer the questions in **English**.

> 王大力（Wang Dali）是中国有名的歌星，我是他的"迷妹"，我从十二岁就开始喜欢他，到现在已经六年了。他虽然唱歌和表演都不太好，但是长得又高又帅，所以我爱他爱得不得了！但是最近他做了非常不好的事，而且很有可能是非常严重的罪行，这让我难过极了。喜欢他浪费了我太多的时间，我以后要花更多时间在学业上。

(1) Who is **Wang Dali**? (1 mark)

(2) How old is **Wu Yue** now? (1 mark)

(3) Why did Wu Yue like **Wang Dali** so much? (1 mark)

(4) What did **Wang Dali** do that made Wu Yue so upset lately? (1 mark)

(5) What is **Wu Yue**'s plan for the future? (1 mark)

6. Translate this paragraph into **English**. Make sure you write the translation in proper English, **NOT** word to word translation. (7 marks)

> 我喜欢吃牛肉面，也喜欢吃鸡肉炒饭。我妈妈做饭非常好吃。每天中午，我在学校吃午饭，我学校的午饭不好吃，但是很健康。

7. Translate this paragraph into **English**. Make sure you write the translation in proper English, **NOT** word to word translation. `Challenge` (7 marks)

> 有时候，我和我的朋友一起去山区散步。周末的时候，我常常在家听音乐，也和我的家人一起看电影。虽然我的作业很多，但是我觉得运动很健康，所以我也常常运动。我最喜欢的运动是在公园跑步。

II. Free Time Activities

Writing

1. You are writing a blog about the celebrity culture. You **must** include the following points:
   » your opinion on having an idol;
   » your own experience of being a fan.

   Write approximately **130-180 Chinese characters**. Challenge (32 marks)

2. Nowadays, more and more people eat out or order takeaways. Write an article to express your opinions. You **must** include the following points:
   » what you think about eating out or ordering takeaway;
   » a recent eating out or ordering takeaway experience;
   » your opinion on healthy lifestyle;
   » any other advice on having a healthy lifestyle.

   Write approximately **150-200 Chinese characters**. (28 marks)

3. Tokyo held the 2020 Olympics in 2021. Write an article to express your opinions. You **must** include the following points:
   » your opinion on holding international events such as Olympics;
   » what people think about doing sports;
   » what sports you and your family or friends did together last week;
   » in the future, what sports you would like to learn.
   Write approximately **150-200 Chinese characters**. Challenge (28 marks)

4. Translate the paragraph into Chinese. Challenge (12 marks)

> I think going to cinema is more interesting than watching TV at home. I often walk to the cinema because it is next to my house and it is so convenient! I went to watch a history film last night and I am going to watch a musical film next Saturday.

III Technology in Everyday Life

 **Listening**

❖ The Internet ❖

1. Three students are interviewed on using the Internet. Listen to each conversation and choose the correct answer for each statement. Write the letters in the blanks.

   (1) He goes online for _____. (1 mark)

A	half an hour every day
B	three times a day
C	three hours every day

   (2) She thinks going online _____. (1 mark)

A	is interesting
B	helps with her study
C	is bad for your eyes

   (3) He normally goes online to _____. (1 mark)

A	watch movies
B	listen to music
C	learn English

Technology Challenge

2. You hear an elderly man talking about his experience with technology on TV. Listen to the whole paragraph and choose **three** correct statements. Write the letters in the boxes.

☐ ☐ ☐ (3 marks)

A	He and his son both live overseas.
B	He used to make expensive phone calls to his son.
C	He learnt to use the Internet and write e-mails.
D	His grandson is studying Chinese in the UK.
E	He often talks to his grandson via WeChat.
F	He thinks technology is convenient and cheap.

Social Media Challenge

3. Four young people, **Zixin** (子欣), **Xiaobai** (小白), **Tingting** (婷婷) and **Meiling** (美玲) are interviewed about using social media. Listen to each person's description and choose a correct option from the table below on what they say about social media. Write the letters in the boxes.

A	Uses social media to do business.
B	To make new friends and learn about different cultures.
C	To help deal with stress and loneliness.
D	Is curious about what social media might be like.
E	Distracts students from studying.
F	Young people should use less social media and read more books.

(1) Zixin ☐ (1 mark)

(2) Xiaobai ☐ (1 mark)

(3) Tingting ☐ (1 mark)

(4) Meiling ☐ (1 mark)

 **Speaking**

◆ **Situation-based test**

Topic: Technology Challenge

For teachers

» The teacher will start the conversation by greeting and introducing his/her role.
» The teacher can only read out the questions listed below in order and the questions cannot be repeated more than twice.

You are interviewed by the school magazine about technology and social media.

1	你通常用什么上网？ Allow the candidate to answer.
2	你觉得社交媒体有什么好处？ **(Two details)** Allow the candidate to answer.
3	你能说出一个用社交媒体的坏处吗？ Allow the candidate to answer.
4	☺! surprising question 最近你上网做了什么？ Allow the candidate to answer.
5	☺? a question Allow the candidate to ask you if you like shopping online. *Answer briefly.*

III. Technology in Everyday Life

Topic: Technology

For candidates

You are interviewed by the school magazine about technology and social media.

» Your teacher will start the conversation by greeting you and introducing his/her role.
» You will answer the following five questions in order.
» The question ☺! is an unprepared question.
» The question ☺? is a question you need to ask your teacher.

---

1. Say what you often use to go online.
2. Say what advantages social media has. (**two details**)
3. Give one negative aspect of using social media.
4. ☺!
5. ☺?
   Ask if the journalist likes shopping online.

◆ **Picture-based test**

Topic: Free time activity

For teachers

» The speaking task should last for **two minutes**.
» The teacher should ask the exact questions listed below in order, and may repeat or paraphrase the questions with similar meaning if needed.

1. 照片里有什么？
2. 你喜欢去电影院看电影吗？为什么？
3. 你最喜欢的电影明星是谁？为什么？
4. 你昨天晚上看电视了吗？
5. 你觉得看电视更有意思还是看电影更有意思？为什么？

III. Technology in Everyday Life

Topic: Free time activity

For candidates

» Write all your notes on a separate A4 paper.
» Answer the following questions in order.
» You can ask your teacher to repeat questions.
» ☺! means you will answer an unprepared question.

Look at the photo and prepare to answer the following questions in order:

1. Describe the photo;
2. Whether you like watching films in the cinema and the reasons;
3. Who your favourite movie star is and the reason.
4. ☺!
5. ☺!

Two-way discussion questions

Using Internet

1. 你经常上网吗？一般在网上做什么？ (2 marks)

2. 你一般用什么社交媒体？ (2 marks)

3. 你有网友吗？你和他/她多久/多长时间联系一次？怎么联系？ (2 marks)

4. 你觉得用社交媒体有什么好处和坏处？ (5 marks)

5. 你有手机吗？你通常用手机做什么？ (2 marks)

6. 你觉得手机有什么优点和缺点？ (3 marks)

7. 你上次用手机是什么时候？你做了什么？ (2 marks)

8. 你更喜欢看电影还是看电视？为什么？ (3 marks)

 Reading

→ Social Media Challenge ←

1. **Wang Ming** (王明) is talking about his experience on using social media.

    Write **T** if the statement is **true**,

    F if the statement is **false**,

    or **N/A** if the statement is **not** mentioned in the text.

> 最近，我的考试成绩非常差，我的父母特别生气。他们说是因为我花太多时间在社交媒体上和朋友聊天儿，所以我不应该用网络了。但是我不同意，我觉得是因为这次的考试题太难了！而且，如果不能上网，我怎么看新闻、做作业？

(1) **Wang Ming**'s recent exam results are very good. ☐ (1 mark)

(2) **Wang Ming** thinks the reason is that the exam questions were very easy. ☐ (1 mark)

(3) **Wang Ming**'s parents are angry about his exam results. ☐ (1 mark)

(4) **Wang Ming**'s parents think that he spends too much time on social media. ☐ (1 mark)

(5) **Wang Ming** has decided not to watch news online anymore. ☐ (1 mark)

→ Technology and Social Media Challenge

2. A group of young people are discussing the use of Internet and social media in a chat room online. Read the statements and choose the correct option for each question. Write the letters in the boxes.

(1) 我从来不用电脑上网，因为用手机上网真是太方便了！
How does this person go on Internet? ☐ (1 mark)

A	Desktop
B	Laptop
C	Mobile phone

(2) 总是看手机，让我的头和脖子都特别疼，我打算少用手机了。
Why does this person decide to use her mobile phone less? ☐ (1 mark)

A	Her parents are not happy about it.
B	Her head and neck are in pain.
C	Her shoulders and neck are in pain.

(3) 我从早到晚在社交媒体上聊天儿，所以最近我的学习成绩下降了。
When does this person use social media? ☐ (1 mark)

A	In the morning
B	In the evening
C	Whole day long

(4) 社交媒体让我能和世界各地的人交朋友，让我的生活更有意思了！
Why does this person say that social media has made life more interesting? ☐
(1 mark)

A	Because he can make friends with people from all over the world.
B	Because he can make friends with people from some special places.
C	Because it makes it easier to make new friends.

III. Technology in Everyday Life

 **Writing**

1. You are writing to your Chinese friend about social media, Internet and technology used in the UK. You **must** include the following points:
   » popular social media used by teenagers in the UK;
   » positive and negative aspects of using social media;
   » two things you did online recently;
   » your plan for the coming weekend.
   Write about **80 Chinese characters**. (16 marks)

2. You are writing on Weibo (微博, the equivalent of twitter in China) about watching films in the cinema. You **must** include the following points:
   » how often you go to the cinema;
   » positive and negative aspects of your local cinemas;
   » your recent cinema experience;
   » your plan for next weekend.
   Write about **120-150 Chinese characters**. Challenge (16 marks)

3. You are writing an article for a Chinese E-magazine for young people about social media. You **must** include the following points:

   » your opinion of social media;

   » your experience of using social media recently.

   Write approximately **120-150 Chinese characters** Challenge (32 marks)

III. Technology in Everyday Life

4. Translate these sentences into **Chinese**.

   (1) I often chat online with my friends. (2 marks)

   (2) Last month I bought a new computer. (2 marks)

   (3) I don't play computer games because it is boring. (2 marks)

   (4) Shopping online is convenient and cheap. (2 marks)

   (5) I use a computer to do my homework. (2 marks)

5. Translate the paragraph into **Chinese**. Challenge

> I am going to study computing in university this September. Since I was a child, I have loved computers and the Internet. I thought it was so interesting and useful. When I was 15, my parents bought me my first computer. I not only use it to do homework and chat with friends online, but also use it to learn about new things and new cultures. (12 marks)

IV Customs and Festivals

🎧 Listening

✧ Festivals ✧

Xiaoli (小丽) is talking about festivals. Listen to the whole paragraph and answer the questions in English.

(1) Why is **Xiaoli**'s favourite festival Chinese New Year? (1 mark)

(2) What do families do on Chinese New Year's Eve? (1 mark)

(3) Name any **two** foods that families have on Chinese New Year's Eve. (2 marks)

(4) Name any **three** things people do to celebrate Chinese New Year. (3 marks)

 **Speaking**

◆ **Situation-based test**

Topic: Festivals Challenge

For teachers

» The teacher will start the conversation by greeting and introducing his/her role.
» The teacher can only read out the questions listed below in order and the questions cannot be repeated more than twice.

You are talking to an exchange student from the UK about festivals during Chinese New Year.

1	圣诞节你会吃什么? Allow the candidate to answer.
2	☺ ! surprising question 去年圣诞节的时候你做了什么? Allow the candidate to answer.
3	今年春节你想怎么过? Allow the candidate to answer.
4	☺ ? a question Allow the candidate to ask what food Chinese people eat during Chinese New Year. *Answer briefly.*
5	☺ ? a question Allow the candidate to ask if Chinese people wear new clothes for Chinese New Year. *Answer briefly.*

IV. Customs and Festivals

Topic: Festivals Challenge

For candidates

You are talking to an exchange student from UK about festivals during Chinese New Year.

» Your teacher will start the conversation by greeting you and introducing his/her role.
» You will answer the following five questions in order.
» The question ☺! is an unprepared question.
» The question ☺? is a question you need to ask your teacher.

---

1. Say what you eat for Christmas.
2. ☺!
3. Say how you plan to celebrate this coming Chinese New Year.
4. ☺?
   Ask what food Chinese people normally eat during Chinese New Year.
5. ☺?
   Ask if Chinese people wear new clothes for Chinese New Year.

Two-way discussion questions

Western and Chinese festivals

1. 你最喜欢的节日是什么？为什么？ (2 marks)

2. 你和你的家人去年是怎么过圣诞节的？ (3 marks)

3. 你希望明年的圣诞节有什么不一样？ (3 marks)

4. 你听说过中国的春节吗？中国人一般怎么过春节？ (2 marks)

5. 你和你的家人庆祝过春节吗？你们去年是怎么过的？ (3 marks)

6. 明年春节你希望你的学校怎么庆祝？ (2 marks)

IV. Customs and Festivals

Reading

1. A brochure describes the festivals in China. Read it and choose between **Chinese New Year**, **Dragon Boat Festival** and **Mid-Autumn Day** to complete each sentence. You can use each festival more than once. Challenge

春节
- 全国放假七天
- 家人一起吃饭：北方人吃饺子，南方人吃汤圆，人们还要吃鱼，因为"年年有余"
- 每个人都要穿新衣服
- 孩子们会放鞭炮
- 去亲戚朋友家拜年
- 举行舞龙和舞狮等庆祝活动

端午节
- 农历五月五日
- 纪念诗人屈原
- 有龙舟比赛
- 人们会吃粽子

中秋节
- 农历八月十五日
- 工作的人要回家看爸爸妈妈
- 家人在一起吃月饼、看月亮

(1) During _____, people are off work for a week. (1 mark)

(2) _____ is on the 5th of May according to the Lunar calendar. (1 mark)

(3) People wear new clothes for _____. (1 mark)

(4) On _____, people watch the moon. (1 mark)

(5) *Zongzi* is the food for _____. (1 mark)

(6) Dragon dance and lion dance is for celebrating _____. (1 mark)

2. Translate this paragraph into **English**. Make sure you write the translation in proper English, **NOT** word to word translation. `Challenge` (7 marks)

> 每年圣诞节，我和我的家人都会一起坐飞机去伦敦，因为我的爷爷奶奶住在伦敦。过圣诞节的时候，我们会一起吃火鸡，送礼物。去年，我的爷爷送了我一个新手机，我非常喜欢。今年，我希望爷爷送我一辆自行车。

IV. Customs and Festivals

 **Writing**

1. You took this photo during Chinese New Year and posted it on social media. Describe this photo and give your opinion on festivals.

   Write approximately **30-40 Chinese characters**. (12 marks)

2. You are writing an e-mail to a friend living in Britain about your plan for the imminent Chinese New Year. You **must** include the following points:
   » the importance of Chinese New Year in China;
   » what you normally eat for this festival;
   » what activities you did for the last Chinese New Year;
   » what you plan to do for the coming Chinese New Year.

   Write approximately **90-120 Chinese characters**. Challenge (20 marks)

GCSE Chinese Practice Workbook and Papers

3. There are more and more young people celebrating traditional festivals in new ways, such as celebrating with friends while travelling rather than having a family reunion dinner. Businesses are making new promotions and sales for the festivals as well. Write an article to express your opinions. You **must** include the following points:

   » compare the traditional and new ways of celebrating Chinese New Year **or** Christmas;
   » which way you prefer **and** why;
   » how you celebrated Chinese New Year **or** Christmas last year;
   » what are your plans for the coming Chinese New Year **or** Christmas.

   Use proper Chinese letter format and give opinions and justifications.
   Write approximately **180-200 Chinese characters.** Challenge   (28 marks)

IV. Customs and Festivals

4. Translate these sentences into **Chinese**.

   (1) I like festivals. (2 marks)

   (2) I eat dumplings. (2 marks)

   (3) Christmas is on the 25th of December. (2 marks)

(4) Chinese people celebrate Chinese New Year. (3 marks)

(5) Chinese people give red envelopes for Chinese New Year. (3 marks)

5. Translate the paragraph into **Chinese**. Challenge

> I like festivals because festivals are fun. I don't go to school during many festivals. I can eat lots of delicious food and I can get presents. Last Christmas, my mum and dad gave me a computer. Next week is Chinese New Year. My grandparents will give me a red envelope. I like red envelopes.
>
> (12 marks)

V Where You Live

🎧 Listening

❖ At the Tube Station *Challenge*

1. Lanlan (兰兰) is asking for help to find places. Listen to the recording and choose the right answer to complete each statement. Write the letters in the blanks.

	Place
A	cinema
B	park
C	bus stop
D	school

	Location
E	in front of the tube station
F	to the right of the tube station
G	to the left of the park
H	right next to the park

(1) The first place **Lanlan** is looking for is the _____. The location of this place is _____.

(2 marks)

(2) The second place **Lanlan** is looking for is the _____. The location of this place is _____.

(2 marks)

66 GCSE Chinese Practice Workbook and Papers

✦ My Community `Challenge` ✦

2. A girl, **Yanyan** (燕燕), and a boy, **Luo Jun** (罗俊), are talking about where they live. Listen to their descriptions and write **one** advantage and **one** disadvantage mentioned by them in **English**.

    (1) **Yanyan**
    Advantage: _____ (1 mark)
    Disadvantage: _____ (1 mark)

    (2) **Luo Jun**
    Advantage: _____ (1 mark)
    Disadvantage: _____ (1 mark)

✦ Around My Living Area ✦

3. **Li Ming** (李明) is talking about the place where he lives. Listen to the whole paragraph and answer the questions in **English**.

    (1) How does **Li Ming** describe the area where he lives? Give **two details**. (2 marks)

    (2) Where does **Li Ming** run? (1 mark)

    (3) How far is **Li Ming**'s school from his home? (1 mark)

✦ House ✦

4. **Li Fang** (李芳) is talking about her house. Listen to her description and choose three correct statements. Write the letters in the boxes. ☐ ☐ ☐ (3 marks)

A	**Li Fang**'s house has two bedrooms.
B	**Li Fang** has a very beautiful garden.
C	**Li Fang**'s house doesn't have study room.
D	**Li Fang**'s little sister's bedroom is the smallest one.

E	**Li Fang**'s family read and drink tea in the garden during the weekend.
F	**Li Fang** does her homework in her bedroom.
G	**Li Fang** would like to move to a bigger house.

❖ Go Shopping ❖

5. **Lili** (丽丽) is talking about a department store near her house. Listen to her description and choose a word/phrase from the box to complete each sentence. There are more words/phrases than blanks.

first	second	chicken	Lili's birthday	third
Christmas	rulers	fourth	trousers	mobile phone
beef	pens	Chinese New Year	dress	stationery

(1) Clothes are on the _____ floor. (1 mark)

(2) On the first floor, you can buy _____ and _____. (2 marks)

(3) **Lili** and her little brother like to visit the _____ floor. (1 mark)

(4) Next week, **Lili**'s parents will buy a _____ for her as it will be _____.

(2 marks)

❖ Shopping ❖

6. **Daming** (大明), **Xiaoli** (小丽), **Ma Tian** (马田) and **Meimei** (美美) are talking about shopping. Listen to the recording and choose the right answer. Write the letters in the blanks.

(1) **Daming** bought _____ yesterday. (1 mark)

A	food
B	clothes
C	stationery
D	books

(2) **Xiaoli** pays by _____ for the clothes.　　　　　　　　　　　　(1 mark)

A	cash
B	her mum's credit card
C	her credit card
D	her dad's credit card

(3) **Ma Tian** goes to a supermarket to buy food because _____.　　　(1 mark)

A	he likes the supermarket
B	he can pay with his credit card
C	the food is cheap
D	the food is fresh

(4) **Meimei** found that it was _____ to buy a computer online.　　　(1 mark)

A	easy
B	cheap
C	expensive
D	safe

❖ Daily Routine ❖

7. **Xiaolin** (小林) is interviewing an English student **David** (大卫) and a Chinese student **Shanshan** (珊珊) about their daily routines. Listen to the conversation **Part A and B individually** and answer the following questions in **English**.

   Part A

   (1) What time does **David** start his first lesson?　　　　　　　　　　　(1 mark)

   (2) How many lessons does **David** have in one day?　　　　　　　　　(1 mark)

(3) What is **David**'s favourite subject? (1 mark)

(4) What is **David**'s plan for the future? (1 mark)

Part B

(5) How many subjects does **Shanshan** have? (1 mark)

(6) What time does **Shanshan** finish school? (1 mark)

(7) What after school activity does **Shanshan** have? (1 mark)

(8) How long does **Shanshan** spend on her homework? (1 mark)

 Speaking

◆ **Situation-based test 1**

Topic: Living area

For teachers

» The teacher will start the conversation by greeting and introducing his/her role.
» The teacher can only read out the questions listed below in order and the questions cannot be repeated more than twice.

Your neighbour just moved to this area. You are talking to your neighbour about the area you live in.

1	你好，请问超市在哪儿？ Allow the candidate to answer.
2	如果我想运动，我应该去哪儿？ Allow the candidate to answer.
3	这附近环境怎么样？ Allow the candidate to answer.
4	☺! surprising question 这附近有中国饭店吗？ Allow the candidate to answer.
5	☺? a question Allow the candidate to ask if they like living in countryside. *Answer briefly.*

V. Where You Live

Topic: Living area

For candidates

Your neighbour just moved to this area. You are talking to your neighbour about the area you live in.

» Your teacher will start the conversation by greeting you and introducing his/her role.
» You will answer the following five questions in order.
» The question ☺! is an unprepared question.
» The question ☺? is a question you need to ask your teacher.

---

1. Say where the supermarket is.
2. Say where you can go to do exercises or sports.
3. Say what the area is like.
4. ☺!
5. ☺?
   Ask if your neighbour likes living in countryside.

◆ **Situation-based test 2**

Topic: My house `Challenge`

For teachers

» The teacher will start the conversation by greeting and introducing his/her role.
» The teacher can only read out the questions listed below in order and the questions cannot be repeated more than twice.

You are talking to your friend about your house.

1	你家住在哪儿？ Allow the candidate to answer.
2	你家附近有什么？ **(two details)** Allow the candidate to answer.
3	你觉得你家的房子怎么样？ Allow the candidate to answer.
4	☺! surprising question 你将来想住在哪儿？为什么？ Allow the candidate to answer.
5	☺? a question Allow the candidate to ask you what kind of house you like. *Answer briefly.*

V. Where You Live

Topic: My house Challenge

For candidates

You are talking to your friend about your house.

» Your teacher will start the conversation by greeting you and introducing his/her role.
» You will answer the following five questions in order.
» The question ☺! is an unprepared question.
» The question ☺? is a question you need to ask your teacher.

1. Say where your house is.
2. Say what facilities there are near your house. (**two details**)
3. Say what you think of your house.
4. ☺!
5. ☺?
   Ask your friend what kind of house they like.

◆ **Situation-based test 3**

Topic: Shopping online `Challenge`

For teachers

» The teacher will start the conversation by greeting and introducing his/her role.
» The teacher can only read out the questions listed below in order and the questions cannot be repeated more than twice.

You are talking to your friend about your online shopping experience.

1	你最近买了什么？ Allow the candidate to answer.
2	你一般会上网买什么？ Allow the candidate to answer.
3	你觉得上网买东西有什么好处和坏处？ Allow the candidate to answer.
4	☺! surprising question 除了上网，你还喜欢去哪儿买东西？ Allow the candidate to answer.
5	☺? a question Allow the candidate to ask if you think shopping online is safe. *Answer briefly.*

V. Where You Live

Topic: Shopping online

For candidates

You are talking to your friend about your online shopping experience.

» Your teacher will start the conversation by greeting you and introducing his/her role.
» You will answer the following five questions in order.
» The question ☺! is an unprepared question.
» The question ☺? is a question you need to ask your teacher.

---

1. Say what you bought recently.
2. Say what you normally buy online.
3. Say what you think the advantages and disadvantages of online shopping are.
4. ☺!
5. ☺?
   Ask if your friend thinks shopping online is safe.

◆ **Situation-based test 4**

Topic: Buying furniture

For teachers

» The teacher will start the conversation by greeting and introducing his/her role.
» The teacher can only read out the questions listed below in order and the questions cannot be repeated more than twice.

You are in a department store in China. You want to buy a bed for your bedroom. You are talking to one of the sales assistants.

1	你好，你想买什么？ Allow the candidate to answer.
2	你想买什么颜色的床？ Allow the candidate to answer.
3	除了床，你还想买什么吗？ Allow the candidate to answer.
4	☺! surprising question 你想用现金还是信用卡支付？ Allow the candidate to answer.
5	☺? a question Allow the candidate to ask where to buy a TV. *Answer briefly.*

V. Where You Live

Topic: Buying furniture

For candidates

You are in a department store in China. You want to buy a bed for your bedroom. You are talking to one of the sales assistants.

» Your teacher will start the conversation by greeting you and introducing his/her role.
» You will answer the following five questions in order.
» The question ☺! is an unprepared question.
» The question ☺? is a question you need to ask your teacher.

1. You would like to buy a bed.
2. Say what colour of bed you would like to buy.
3. Say what else you would like to buy apart from the bed.
4. ☺!
5. ☺?
   Ask the sales assistant where to buy a TV.

◆ **Picture-based test 1**

Topic: Home

For teachers

» The speaking task should last for **two minutes**.
» The teacher should ask the exact questions listed below in order, and may repeat or paraphrase the questions with similar meaning if needed.

1. 照片里有什么？
2. 你怎么看和兄弟或姐妹住同一间房间？
3. 上个周末你在家做了什么？
4. 你喜欢你住的地方吗？为什么？
5. 说说你家的房子。

Topic: Home

For candidates

» Write all your notes on a separate A4 paper.
» Answer the following questions in order.
» You can ask your teacher to repeat questions.
» ☺! means you will answer an unprepared question.

Look at the photo and prepare to answer the following questions in order:

1. Describe the photo;
2. What you think about sharing a room with a sibling;
3. What you did at home last weekend;
4. ☺!
5. ☺!

◆ **Picture-based test 2**

Topic: Home Challenge

For teachers

» The speaking task should last for **three minutes**.
» The teacher should ask the exact questions listed below in order, and may repeat or paraphrase the questions with similar meaning if needed.

1. 照片里有什么？
2. 你怎么看和兄弟或姐妹住同一间房间？
3. 上个周末你在家做了什么？
4. 将来你想和父母一起住还是自己住？为什么？
5. 你喜欢你住的地方吗？为什么？

V. Where You Live

Topic: Home Challenge

For candidates

» Write all your notes on a separate A4 paper.
» Answer the following questions in order.
» You can ask your teacher to repeat questions.
» ☺! means you will answer an unprepared question.

Look at the photo and prepare to answer the following questions in order:

1. Describe the photo;
2. What you think about sharing a room with a sibling;
3. What you did at home last weekend;
4. ☺!
5. ☺!

◆ **Picture-based test 3**

Topic: My house

For teachers

» The speaking task should last **two-and-a-half to three minutes**.
» The teacher should ask the exact questions listed below in order, and cannot repeat the questions more than twice.
» The teacher can ask follow up questions using "还有呢？" and "为什么？" to prompt extended answers.

1. 描述这张照片。（还有呢？）
2. 你上一次在你家厨房做了什么好吃的？（还有呢？）
3. 你喜欢做饭还是买外卖？为什么？（还有呢？）
4. 描述你的家。（还有呢？）
5. 你希望你将来的家是什么样的？（还有呢？）

Topic: My house

For candidates

» Write all your notes on a separate A4 paper.
» Answer the following questions in order.
» You can ask your teacher to repeat questions.

Look at the photo and prepare to answer the following questions in order:
1. Describe the photo;
2. What food you made last time in your kitchen;
3. You prefer cooking or having takeaway and the reasons;
4. Talk about your house;
5. What you would like your future home to look like.

◆ **Picture-based test 4**

Topic: Place I live Challenge

For teachers

» The speaking task should last **three to three-and-a-half minutes**.
» The teacher should ask the exact questions listed below in order, and cannot repeat the questions more than twice.
» The teacher can ask follow up questions using "还有呢？" and "为什么？" to prompt extended answers.

1. 描述这张照片。（还有呢？）
2. 你住的地方环境怎么样？（还有呢？）
3. 说说你最近在家附近做了什么运动？（还有呢？）
4. 你以后想住在什么样的地方？（为什么？还有呢？）
5. 你喜欢住在热闹的地方还是安静的地方？（为什么？）

V. Where You Live

Topic: Place I live

For candidates

» Write all your notes on a separate A4 paper.
» Answer the following questions in order.
» You can ask your teacher to repeat questions.
» ☺! means you will answer an unprepared question.

Look at the photo and prepare to answer the following questions in order:

1. Describe the photo;
2. How your living area is;
3. What sports you did recently in your community area;
4. Where you would like to live in the future.
5. ☺!

◆ **Picture-based test 5**

Topic: Shopping

For teachers

» The speaking task should last **two-and-a-half to three minutes**.
» The teacher should ask the exact questions listed below in order, and cannot repeat the questions more than twice.
» The teacher can ask follow up questions using "还有呢？" and "为什么？" to prompt extended answers.

1. 描述这张照片。（还有呢？）
2. 你上次去百货商场买了什么？（为什么？还有呢？）
3. 你喜欢在网上买东西还是在商店买东西？（为什么？还有呢？）
4. 下次生日你想买什么作为生日礼物？（为什么？）
5. 你家附近有什么商店？（还有呢？）

V. Where You Live

Topic: Shopping

For candidates

» Write all your notes on a separate A4 paper.
» Answer the following questions in order.
» You can ask your teacher to repeat questions.

Look at the photo and prepare to answer the following questions in order:
1. Describe the photo;
2. What you bought in the department store last time;
3. If you like to shop online or shop in shops;
4. What gift you would like to buy for your next birthday;
5. What kind of shops there are near your house.

Two-way discussion questions

My neighbourhood

1. 你住在什么样的地方?（农村、小镇还是大城市?） (2 marks)
2. 你家附近的环境怎么样? (2 marks)
3. 你家附近有什么好玩儿的地方? (2 marks)
4. 你家离……远吗? (3 marks)
5. 从你家去……怎么走? (3 marks)
6. 你通常在哪儿和你的朋友见面?为什么? (3 marks)
7. 长大以后，你想留在你的家乡吗?为什么? (2 marks)
8. 你家大吗?有几个卧室? (2 marks)
9. 你家有……吗? (1 mark)
10. 你最喜欢你家里的什么地方? (2 marks)
11. 你上次打扫你的卧室是什么时候? (1 mark)
12. 你经常（邀）请朋友去你家玩吗?为什么? (2 marks)

V. Where You Live

 **Reading**

✧ Our Community ✧

1. Some young people are describing their community. Read the passage below and write the correct letter of the places they have for each person.

> 兰兰（Lanlan）：
> 我家旁边有足球场，也有游泳池。
>
> 丽丽（Lili）：
> 我家后边有一个大图书馆。
>
> 军军（Junjun）：
> 我家附近就是火车站和购物中心。

A	swimming pool
B	school
C	library
D	shopping centre
E	cinema
F	museum

(1) **Lanlan** ☐ (1 mark)

(2) **Lili** ☐ (1 mark)

(3) **Junjun** ☐ (1 mark)

My House `Challenge`

2. Read the description from three students about their new houses.

> 兰兰（Lanlan）：
> 　　我家在伦敦郊区。我家的房子很大，有三个卧室。花园是我最喜欢的地方。
>
> 大海（Dahai）：
> 　　我家在北京。我家的房子不太大，只有两个卧室和一个浴室。我很喜欢花园，可是城市里有花园的房子太贵了。
>
> 庆林（Qinglin）：
> 　　我家在巴黎农村。我家的房子又大又好看，有五个卧室和两个浴室。我家有一个花园，花园里有一个游泳池。我家的厨房也很大，妈妈最喜欢在厨房里做饭。有时候我也会帮妈妈做饭。

Who do the following statements apply to?
Tick **L** if the statement only applies to **Lanlan**,
　　D if the statement only applies to **Dahai**,
　　Q if the statement only applies to **Qinglin**,
or **multiple boxes** if the statement **applies to more than one person**.

(1) I have no garden in the house. (1 mark)

　　L ☐　　D ☐　　Q ☐

(2) I live in the countryside. (1 mark)

　　L ☐　　D ☐　　Q ☐

(3) There are three bedrooms in my house. (1 mark)

　　L ☐　　D ☐　　Q ☐

(4) I help with cooking in the kitchen. (1 mark)

　　L ☐　　D ☐　　Q ☐

(5) I like the garden. (1 mark)

L ☐   D ☐   Q ☐

◆ My New Home `Challenge` ◆

3. **Xiaomei** (小美) has written a letter to **Fangfang** (芳芳) about her new home. Read the letter below and answer the questions in **English**.

> 芳芳：
> 　　你好!
> 　　你最近怎么样？还好吗？
> 　　我这个星期搬了新家，从伦敦搬到了伦敦西边的农村。这里比伦敦安静很多。我家后边是森林，前边是一个湖。我周末可以去森林里骑自行车，早上可以听到鸟叫，晚上还可以看到星星。这里太漂亮了！
> 　　不过，这儿没有伦敦方便。火车站离我家开车十分钟。可是我没有车，所以我每天早上要骑自行车去火车站，再坐火车去工作。下雨的时候，我就会坐出租车回家。
> 　　但是，我还是非常喜欢我的新家。你觉得住在城市好还是住在农村好？等你回信！
> 　　　　　　　　　　　　　　　　　　　　　　　　　　小美

(1) Where did **Xiaomei** move to? (1 mark)

(2) What is there in front of **Xiaomei**'s new home? (1 mark)

(3) What does **Xiaomei** plan to do at the weekend? (1 mark)

(4) How far is **Xiaomei**'s new house away from the train station? (1 mark)

(5) When it rains, how does **Xiaomei** travel home from work? (1 mark)

(6) According to **Xiaomei**, give two details comparing her new house with living in London. (2 marks)

①
②

❖ My Home ❖

4. Read the following statements from **Meimei** (美美), **Li Shan** (李山), **Xiaoli** (小丽) and **Daming** (大明) about their homes. Write **Meimei, Li Shan, Xiaoli** or **Daming** in the blanks to complete the sentences. You can use each name more than once.

> 美美：我的卧室很干净，有一张床、一张桌子、两把椅子和一个电脑，我有时候在卧室里玩电脑游戏。我的卧室里没有电视。
>
> 李山：我家不大也不小，有两个卧室、一个客厅、一个厨房和两个厕所。我爸爸妈妈的卧室比我的卧室大很多。
>
> 小丽：我住在市中心。我家不太大，但是有一个花园，我常常和我的爸爸在花园里做运动。我家没有书房，所以我在客厅做作业。
>
> 大明：我和我的爸爸妈妈还有一个弟弟住在一个大房子里。我家有两层，我的卧室在楼上，我弟弟的卧室在我卧室的旁边，我爸爸妈妈的卧室在楼下。

(1) _____ plays computer games in the bedroom. (1 mark)

(2) _____ does homework in the living room. (1 mark)

(3) _____ has two toilets in the house. (1 mark)

(4) _____ and his younger brother's bedrooms are on the same floor. (1 mark)

(5) _____ 's bedroom is smaller than his parents'. (1 mark)

(6) _____ does sports in the garden. (1 mark)

(7) _____ lives in the city centre. (1 mark)

◆ My Living Areas Challenge ◆

5. **Lili** (丽丽), **Xiaoli** (小李), **Dashan** (大山) and **Nana** (娜娜) are describing their living areas. Read their descriptions and choose the right answer for each statement or question. Write the letters in the blanks.

丽丽：我家住在农村。那里又安静又漂亮，有很多树和很多花，人很少。我家附近有一个学校和一个商店。我每天走路去学校。

小李：我和我的家人住在伦敦市中心。那里很热闹，有很多人，也有很多商店，买东西非常方便。我家前面是一个运动中心，后面是一个大超市，我家离银行和邮局不远。

大山：我的家在城市。因为城市很小，有很多人，所以很不干净。周围有很多垃圾，环境不好。以后，我想去一个漂亮的地方住。

娜娜：我住在海边，因为我喜欢大海。周末的时候，我常常去海边散步、遛狗。我喜欢我住的环境，不但很干净，而且离火车站很近，我去旅行很方便。

(1) In **Lili**'s living area, there is **not** a lot of _____ . (1 mark)

A	trees
B	flowers
C	people
D	shops

(2) Behind **Xiaoli**'s house, there is a _____ . (1 mark)

A	sports centre
B	supermarket
C	bank
D	post office

(3) Which comment is from **Dashan** about his living area? _____ (1 mark)

A	Satisfied
B	Not satisfied
C	Love it
D	Neither satisfied nor unsatisfied

(4) Which one below is **NOT** how **Nana** thinks about her living area? _____

(1 mark)

A	Clean
B	Convenient
C	Like it
D	Very small

Answer the following questions in **English**.

(5) How does **Lili** go to school? (1 mark)

(6) What can **Nana** do in her living area? (1 mark)

V. Where You Live

Daily Routine Challenge

6. Four people comment on their daily routines.

明明（Mingming）：

　　我每天六点四十五分起床，七点半吃完早饭就去上学。在学校我有六节课。中午，我和我的朋友一起吃午饭。午饭我吃鸡肉、米饭，我的朋友吃比萨。下午放学以后，我回家做作业。吃完晚饭以后，我有时候会看电视，有时候玩电脑游戏。

小丽（Xiaoli）：

　　我今天开始放暑假。我想每天九点起床，然后去公园跑步，十点回家吃早饭。因为天气很热，所以下午我要和朋友一起游泳。有时候，我会帮妈妈做晚饭，我会做三明治和鱼。

大山（Dashan）：

　　今天是星期一，早上我有两节英语课和两节科学课。我非常喜欢英语课，因为英语老师很有意思。下午一点二十分，我有两节体育课。今天我们要打网球，我不会打网球，但是我的爸爸说打网球很好玩儿。

美美（Meimei）：

　　我的日常生活很忙，每天早上，我要去遛狗，然后开始在网上工作，有时候，我也会在网上开会。工作结束以后，我在家做饭，有时候我会去商店买东西，但是我喜欢在网上买东西，因为在网上买东西很方便，而且很快，我用信用卡买东西也很安全。

Fill in the blanks to complete the sentences. Write the words in the blanks.

(1) **Mingming** eats _____ for lunch. (1 mark)

(2) **Xiaoli** gets up at 9 am because _____ . (1 mark)

(3) **Dashan** has _____ lessons on Monday. (please enter a number) (1 mark)

(4) **Meimei** prefers to shop _____ because it is convenient. (1 mark)

Answer the following questions in **English**.

(5) What does **Mingming** sometimes do after dinner? (1 mark)

(6) What does **Meimei** do after she walks her dog? (1 mark)

·› Shopping Challenge ‹·

7. Read the passage below about shopping.

在中国，人们常说"吃穿住行"，说的是在我们的生活中，吃饭、穿的衣服、住的房子和出行都是非常重要的。以前，人们去百货商场买衣服，那里有什么衣服你就买什么衣服。现在越来越多的人喜欢在网上买衣服，因为网上有各种各样的衣服，而且很便宜。以前，人们买衣服是因为要保暖，现在人们买衣服是因为要时尚、漂亮。

出行是指你怎么去一个地方。二十年前，人们从北京到上海坐火车要十几个小时，现在坐高铁只要四个多小时，坐飞机只要两个多小时。以前人们坐公共汽车去上班，现在越来越多的人开车去上班。

人们希望吃穿住行越来越好。

» 保暖 (bǎonuǎn)：keep warm

» 高铁 (gāotiě)：high-speed railway

(1) Choose three correct statements and write the letters in the boxes. ☐ ☐ ☐

(3 marks)

A	There isn't a big change in people's lives according to the passage.
B	There are four things mentioned in the passage which are very important to people's life.
C	Now, more and more people do clothes shopping online.
D	In earlier times, people bought clothes because they wanted to be beautiful and fashionable.
E	It took about four hours to get from Beijing to Shanghai by train two decades ago.
F	It takes around two hours to get from Beijing to Shanghai by plane now.
G	According to the passage, more and more people take public transport to work.

Answer the following questions in **English**.

(2) How did people do clothes shopping before? (1 mark)

(3) How long does it take to get from Beijing to Shanghai by high-speed train? (1 mark)

8. Translate the paragraph into **English**. Make sure you write the translation in proper English, **NOT** word to word translation. Challenge

我两年前开始住在英国农村，因为这里不仅风景漂亮，而且环境很好。我和我的家人住在一个大房子里。每天早上，我骑自行车去学校，我的爸爸妈妈开车去上班。晚上吃完饭，我们一起去山区散步。

(7 marks)

9. Translate this paragraph into **English**. Make sure you write the translation in proper English, **NOT** word to word translation. `Challenge`

> 我家的厨房里有桌子、椅子和一个冰箱。我和我的家人不吃肉，但是我们吃鱼。
>
> 冰箱里有很多青菜和水果。每天晚上，我和我的家人一起在厨房吃晚饭。吃完晚饭以后，我在厨房做作业，我爸爸妈妈在客厅看电视。

(7 marks)

 **Writing**

1. Two friends went shopping as shown in the photo below. Imagine you are one of them and describe this photo and give your opinions on the clothes you bought. Write approximately **30-40 Chinese characters**. (12 marks)

2. Your friend sent you his latest photo via WeChat.

Describe what you can see in the photo. Write **four** sentences in **Chinese**.

(1) _____ (2 marks)

(2) _____ (2 marks)

(3) _____ (2 marks)

(4) _____ (2 marks)

3. Write an article about your daily routine. You **must** include the following points:
   » what time your school starts;
   » what lessons you had yesterday;
   » what you do for after school activities;
   » give comments on your daily routine.
   Write approximately **50-60 Chinese characters**. (16 marks)

4. Write a blog about where you live. You **must** include the following points:
   » what rooms there are in your house;
   » positive and negative aspects of your house;
   » the surrounding areas near your house;
   » what improvements you would like to see in your living conditions.
   Write approximately **80 Chinese characters**. (16 marks)

V. Where You Live

5. Write an article to describe your house. You **must** include the following points:
   » what rooms you have in your house;
   » your opinion of your own bedroom;
   » the activity you did with your family last weekend;
   » how you would like to improve your current living conditions.

   Write approximately **100-120 Chinese characters**. (20 marks)

6. You are writing a letter to a Chinese exchange student who is going to stay at your house for 2 weeks. You **must** include the following points:

» your daily routine;

» description of your house;

» the dinner your family had the previous evening;

» the activities you plan to do with this student after his/her arrival.

Use proper Chinese letter format.

Write approximately **150-200 Chinese characters**. Challenge (28 marks)

7. You are writing a letter to your Chinese pen pal about shopping. You **must** include the following points:
   » the shops in your local area;
   » a memorable shopping experience you had recently;
   » your payment method in the mentioned shopping experience and the reasons;
   » your plan for the next shopping trip.
   Use proper Chinese letter format.
   Write approximately **150-200 Chinese characters**. (Challenge) (28 marks)

8. Translate this paragraph into **English**. Make sure you write the translation in proper English, **NOT** word to word translation. Challenge

> 将来我想住在西班牙。两年前我和我男朋友去过西班牙。我觉得西班牙的天气非常好，食物也很好吃。除此以外，西班牙人也十分友好。所以，我希望将来在西班牙一边工作，一边学习西班牙语。

(9 marks)

9. Translate these sentences into **Chinese**.

(1) I like going shopping. (2 marks)

(2) My house is clean. (2 marks)

(3) I eat breakfast at 7 o'clock. (2 marks)

(4) Yesterday, I went to the supermarket. (2 marks)

(5) My school is to the left of my house. (2 marks)

10. Translate the paragraph into **Chinese**. `Challenge`

> I like the place where I live. Near my house, there are all kinds of shops. I think it is very convenient. The environment is very clean. I take the bus to London at the weekend. My house is not far from the city centre.
> (12 marks)

VI Travel and Tourism

 Listening

❖ Weather Forecast ❖

1. You will hear a weather forecast on the radio. Listen to the recording and choose the correct answer for each question. Write the letters in the blanks.

   (1) What's the weather like tomorrow? _____ (1 mark)

A	It's very hot with heavy rain.
B	It's cold with heavy rain.
C	It's hot and sunny.

   (2) What advice is given? _____ (1 mark)

A	Stay indoors
B	Bring an umbrella
C	Enjoy the sun

❖ Hotel ❖

2. **Lanlan** (兰兰) is talking about the hotel she stayed in in Yunnan last August. Listen to the recording and choose the right answer for each question. Write the letters in the blanks.

(1) **Where** is the hotel? _____ (1 mark)

A	Countryside
B	Seaside
C	Mountain area

(2) **What** does she think of the hotel? _____ (1 mark)

A	Quiet
B	Lively
C	Clean

❖ Fangfei's Stay ❖

3. **Fangfei** (芳菲) is talking about the hotel she stayed in in Hangzhou. Listen to the recording and choose the right answer for each question. Write the letters in the blanks.

(1) **Where** is the hotel? _____ (1 mark)

A	City centre
B	Lakeside
C	Town

(2) **What** does she think of the hotel? _____ (1 mark)

A	Beautiful scenery
B	Cold at night
C	Nice restaurant

✧ Holidays Challenge ✧

4. **Tingting** (婷婷) is talking about her holiday last year. Listen to the recording and choose the correct answer for each statement. Write the letters in the blanks.

   (1) **Tingting** went to France in _____ last year.   (1 mark)

A	July
B	August
C	September

   (2) **Tingting** went to France by _____.   (1 mark)

A	ship
B	plane
C	car

   (3) It took them _____ to get there.   (1 mark)

A	half an hour
B	three and a half hours
C	five hours

   (4) They like the journey because _____.   (1 mark)

A	they can enjoy the weather
B	they can enjoy the big ship
C	they can enjoy the sea

✧ Holidays Challenge ✧

5. **Tingting** (婷婷) is talking about her holiday last year. Listen to the paragraph.
   Write **L** if she **likes** the mentioned viewpoint of the holiday,
   　　　D if she **dislikes** the mentioned viewpoint of the holiday,
   　　or **M** if her opinion is **mixed**.

VI. Travel and Tourism

(1) The island ☐ (1 mark)

(2) The people ☐ (1 mark)

(3) The food ☐ (1 mark)

(4) The weather ☐ (1 mark)

⇢ Staying in a Hotel Challenge ⇠

6. **Lanlan** (兰兰) is talking about the hotel she stayed in last August. Listen to the description and answer the questions in **English**.

    (1) Where is the hotel? (1 mark)

    (2) What facilities are there in the hotel? (1 mark)

    (3) What does **Lanlan** think of the hotel? Give two options. (1 mark)

⇢ Holiday Plans Challenge ⇠

7. **Ma Tian** (马田), **Lili** (丽丽), **Xiaoming** (小明) and **Shanshan** (珊珊) are talking about their holiday plans. Listen to the recording.

    Part A

    Choose the right answer for each question. Write the letters in the blanks.

    (1) What is the weather like in Sanya? _____ (1 mark)

A	Windy
B	Cloudy
C	Sunny
D	Rainy

(2) What facility does the hotel have where **Lili** wants to stay have? _____ (1 mark)

A	Swimming pool
B	Bar
C	Gym
D	Tennis court

(3) Why would **Xiaoming** like to go to Spain? _____ (1 mark)

A	Nice weather
B	Nice food
C	The sea is beautiful
D	Less people

(4) How long will **Xiaoming** stay in Spain? _____ (1 mark)

A	5 days
B	A week
C	Two weeks
D	10 days

(5) How many cities will **Shanshan** travel to in China? _____ (1 mark)

A	2
B	3
C	4
D	5

(6) How will **Shanshan** travel from Beijing to Shanghai? _____ (1 mark)

A	By car
B	By ferry
C	By plane
D	By train

VI. Travel and Tourism

Part B

Answer the following question in **English**.

(7) What **two elements** made **Shanshan** decide the way she travels in China? (2 marks)

 **Speaking**

◆ **Situation-based test 1**

Topic: Holiday

For teachers

» The teacher will start the conversation by greeting and introducing his/her role.
» The teacher can only read out the questions listed below in order and the questions cannot be repeated more than twice.

You are talking to your friend about your last holiday.

1	你上一次假期去了哪儿？ Allow the candidate to answer.
2	假期里你做了什么？ **(two details)** Allow the candidate to answer.
3	☺! surprising question 假期时你住在哪儿？ Allow the candidate to answer.
4	你喜欢这次假期吗？为什么？ **(one opinion)** Allow the candidate to answer.
5	☺? a question Allow the candidate to ask you if you like going to France in holiday. *Answer briefly.*

VI. Travel and Tourism

Topic: Holiday

For candidates

You are talking to your friend about your last holiday.

» Your teacher will start the conversation by greeting you and introducing his/her role.
» You will answer the following five questions in order.
» The question ☺! is an unprepared question.
» The question ☺? is a question you need to ask your teacher.

---

1. Say where you went for your last holiday.
2. Say what you did during the holiday. **(two details)**
3. ☺!
4. Say whether you liked this holiday or not and the reason. **(one opinion)**
5. ☺?
   Ask if your friend likes going to France on holiday.

◆ **Situation-based test 2**

Topic: My holiday Challenge

For teachers

» The teacher will start the conversation by greeting and introducing his/her role.
» The teacher can only read out the questions listed below in order and the questions cannot be repeated more than twice.

You are talking to your friend about your last holiday.

1	你上一次假期是什么时候？ Allow the candidate to answer.
2	假期里你做了什么？ **(two details)** Allow the candidate to answer.
3	☺! surprising question 你觉得这次假期怎么样？ **(one opinion)** Allow the candidate to answer.
4	下一次你想去哪儿度假？为什么？ Allow the candidate to answer.
5	☺? a question Allow the candidate to ask you what weather you like when you're on holiday. *Answer briefly.*

VI. Travel and Tourism

Topic: My holiday Challenge

For candidates

You are talking to your friend about your last holiday.

» Your teacher will start the conversation by greeting you and introducing his/her role.

» You will answer the following five questions in order.

» The question ☺! is an unprepared question.

» The question ☺? is a question you need to ask your teacher.

---

1. Say when your last holiday was.
2. Say what you did during the holiday. (**two details**)
3. ☺!
4. Say where you would like to go for a holiday next time and the reason.
5. ☺?
   Ask your friend what kind of weather he/she likes when he's/she's on holiday.

◆ **Picture-based test 1**

Topic: Travel and tourism

For teachers

» The speaking task should last for **two minutes**.
» The teacher should ask the exact questions listed below in order, and may repeat or paraphrase the questions with similar meaning if needed.

1. 照片里有什么？
2. 你最喜欢什么样的假期？为什么？
3. 假期的时候，你喜欢做什么？
4. 假期的时候，英国的天气怎么样？
5. 下一次你想去哪儿度假？

VI. Travel and Tourism

Topic: Travel and tourism

For candidates

» Write all your notes on a separate A4 paper.
» Answer the following questions in order.
» You can ask your teacher to repeat questions.
» ☺! means you will answer an unprepared question.

Look at the photo and prepare to answer the following questions in order:

1. Describe the photo;
2. What kind of holiday you prefer and the reason;
3. What you like to do during holidays;
4. ☺!
5. ☺!

◆ **Picture-based test 2**

Topic: Travel and tourism `Challenge`

For teachers

» The speaking task should last for **three minutes**.
» The teacher should ask the exact questions listed below in order, and may repeat or paraphrase the questions with similar meaning if needed.

1. 照片里有什么？
2. 度假的时候你喜欢住在大酒店还是小旅社？为什么？
3. 疫情前你去哪儿度假了？
4. 度假的时候，你喜欢做什么？
5. 将来你最想去哪儿看看？

Topic: Travel and tourism Challenge

For candidates

» Write all your notes on a separate A4 paper.
» Answer the following questions in order.
» You can ask your teacher to repeat questions.
» ☺! means you will answer an unprepared question.

Look at the photo and prepare to answer the following questions in order:

1. Describe the photo;
2. Whether you prefer to stay in a fancy hotel or hostel during your holiday and the reason;
3. Before the pandemic, where you went for your last holiday.
4. ☺!
5. ☺!

Two-way discussion questions

Travels and trips

1. Nǐmen xuéxiào tōngcháng shénme shíhou fàng shǔjià？
   你们学校 通常 什么时候放暑假？ (1 mark)

2. Nǐ shàng cì qù dùjià shì shénme shíhou？
   你上次去度假是什么时候？ (1 mark)

3. Nǐ qùle nǎr？ Hé shéi yìqǐ qù de？ Hǎowánr ma？
   你去了哪儿？和谁一起去的？好玩儿吗？ (3 marks)

4. Nǐ nàr de tiānqì zěnmeyàng？
   你那儿的天气怎么样？ (2 marks)

5. Nǐ měi cì qù dùjià dōu huì dài yí gè dàdà de lǚxíngxiāng ma？
   你每次去度假都会带一个大大的旅行箱吗？ (2 marks)

6. Nǐ jīnnián shǔjià dǎsuàn qù nǎr dùjià？ Wèishénme？
   你今年暑假打算去哪儿度假？为什么？ (3 marks)

7. Nǐ qùguo Zhōngguó ma？ Nǐ juéde Zhōngguó zěnmeyàng？
   你去过中国吗？你觉得中国怎么样？ (3 marks)

8. Nǐ gèng yuànyì hé jiārén háishi gèng yuànyì gēn péngyou yìqǐ dùjià？ Wèishénme？
   你更愿意和家人还是更愿意跟朋友一起度假？为什么？

   (5 marks)

VI. Travel and Tourism

 **Reading**

✧ Holiday Activities ✧

1. Three friends are talking about what they did on holiday. Read the statements and write the correct letter in each box about what each person did on their holiday.

A	Watched movies
B	Swam in the sea
C	Played football
D	Hiked in the mountains
E	Went horse riding
F	Visited museums

(1) Xiaoming ☐ (1 mark)

(2) Yingzi ☐ (1 mark)

(3) Ziqi ☐ (1 mark)

My Holiday Plan (Challenge)

2. Four friends are talking about their holiday plans. Read the messages below and complete the sentences in **English**. Write the words in the blanks.

> 燕子（Yanzi）
> 六月考试后，我打算和我的好朋友坐火车去山区骑马、画画。

> 蓝心（Lanxin）
> 我想新年的时候去看看爷爷奶奶，他们住在德国。

> 小杰（Xiaojie）
> 我打算去见我的网友。我们在网上认识三个月了，我很喜欢她。

> 小雪（Xiaoxue）
> 我要和爸爸妈妈去美国纽约度假。我们打算参观有名的大学。

(1) **Yanzi** plans to go to the mountains by _____, and she is going to go horse riding and _____. (2 marks)

(2) **Lanxin** wants to visit her grandparents during _____. Her grandparents live in _____. (2 marks)

(3) **Xiaojie** plans to meet his _____, whom he has known for _____. (2 marks)

(4) **Xiaoxue** is going to _____ with her parents, and they plan to visit _____. (2 marks)

Trip Plan Challenge

3. **Amy** will attend a school trip to Beijing next year. She writes to her grandma in Shanghai about the trip. Read the letter below and answer the questions in **English**.

> 亲爱的奶奶：
>   您和爷爷都好吗？我已经两年没有见到你们了，我很想你们。
>   明年七月，学校会组织学习汉语的学生去北京学习和旅游，我也报名参加了。妈妈说学校旅游结束后，我可以去上海看你们。我太高兴了！
>   老师说我们会去长城、故宫、天安门广场，还会去看大熊猫。奶奶，你一定见过大熊猫，它们和电视里一样可爱吗？
>   你可爱的孙女，
>   Amy ☺

(1) For how long has **Amy** not seen her grandma? (1 mark)

(2) When will **Amy** go to Beijing? (1 mark)

(3) Who can join the school trip? (1 mark)

(4) What will **Amy** do after the school trip? (1 mark)

(5) Which places will **Amy** visit in Beijing? (1 mark)

(6) What question does **Amy** ask in the end? (1 mark)

Holiday Experience [Challenge]

4. **Xiaojun** (小军) is talking about his holiday with his dog last Christmas.

   Write **Y** if the statement is **true**,

   N if the statement is **false**,

   or **N/A** if the statement is **not** mentioned in the text.

   > 去年圣诞节，我去了西班牙的一个小岛上度假。这里很安静，比英国暖和很多。我没有结婚，也没有女朋友，所以我是和我的狗一起去的。虽然是十二月，但是海水不太冷。我的狗非常喜欢在海边玩，还会去海里游泳。我不会游泳，但是我喜欢在海边晒太阳。我最喜欢的是吃海鲜，不过我的狗不喜欢海鲜。我吃海鲜的时候，它就不高兴地看着我。

   (1) **Xiaojun** went to Spain in December. ☐ (1 mark)

   (2) **Xiaojun** is single. ☐ (1 mark)

   (3) **Xiaojun** would go swimming in the sea with his dog. ☐ (1 mark)

   (4) Both **Xiaojun** and his dog love seafood. ☐ (1 mark)

   (5) **Xiaojun** often eats seafood. ☐ (1 mark)

VI. Travel and Tourism

Holiday Plans (Challenge)

5. **Xiaomei** (小美) and **David** (大卫) are pen pals. Before the holiday, Xiaomei and David described their holiday plans. Read the letters below.

小美：

你好。

我要放假了。这个冬天，我要去意大利，因为意大利的冬天比英国的冬天好。英国的冬天很冷，而且常常下雨，总是阴天，但是意大利的冬天不冷不热，而且总是晴天。我和我的家人要在一个朋友家里住三天，还要坐火车去一个很漂亮的地方——西西里（Xīxīlǐ）。我们要在酒店住四天，我爸爸提前（tíqián）订了火车票，非常便宜。

我很期待去意大利，除了因为我学了两年意大利语以外，也因为我在意大利有一个好朋友，我想去看看我的好朋友。

你什么时候放假？你放假要做什么？提前祝你圣诞快乐！

大卫
十二月十八日

大卫：

你好。

因为我也要放假了，而且这个学期我很累，所以我和我的家人要去旅行。虽然我住在中国，但是我没去过中国南方，所以这个假期我们要去南方玩，我们打算去广州。之后我们还要去西安，我的妹妹想去西安吃биáng biáng（biángbiáng）面，我想去看兵马俑，我的爸爸妈妈想去买东西。

我希望明年去欧洲旅行。我会说英语和法语，我没去过欧洲，我想去英国和法国。你去过法国吗？那里的天气怎么样？交通方便吗？

祝你圣诞快乐，新年快乐！

小美
十二月二十日

» <ruby>西西里<rt>Xīxīlǐ</rt></ruby>：Sicily

» <ruby>提前<rt>tíqián</rt></ruby>：do sth in advance

» <ruby>biángbiáng 面<rt></rt></ruby>：a kind of noodle in Xi'an (The character is 𰻞, which has the most strokes in Chinese characters. However, this Chinese character cannot be input in the computer.)

Part A

Choose the right answer for each question. Write the letters in the blanks.

(1) Which word below is **NOT** mentioned when describing winter in the UK? _____

(1 mark)

A	Rainy
B	Cloudy
C	Cold
D	Sunny

(2) How will **David** and his family go to Sicily? _____ (1 mark)

A	By plane
B	By train
C	By car
D	By bus

(3) What activity would **Xiaomei** like to do in Xi'an? _____ (1 mark)

A	See terracotta warriors and horses
B	Eat noodles
C	Go shopping
D	Go to the theatre

(4) Where does **Xiaomei** want to travel next year? _____ (1 mark)

A	Asia
B	Europe
C	America
D	Africa

Part B

Answer the following questions in **English**.

(5) What is the weather like in Italy? (1 mark)

(6) What are the two reasons why **David** is looking forward to travelling to Italy? (2 marks)

(7) What are the two reasons why **Xiaomei** will travel to Xi'an and Guangzhou? (2 marks)

6. Translate this paragraph into **English**. Make sure you write the translation in proper English, **NOT** word to word translation. (9 marks)

> 功夫表演是明天晚上八点，在北京电影院。除了功夫表演以外，还有唱歌和舞蹈。门票一个人六十八元。

Writing

1. Your cousin in China sent you the photo below.

   Describe what you can see in the photo. Write **four sentences** in **Chinese**.

   (1) _____ (2 marks)

   (2) _____ (2 marks)

   (3) _____ (2 marks)

   (4) _____ (2 marks)

2. You are going to take a school trip to China. Write a short letter to your Chinese friend about the imminent trip. You **must** include the points below:
   » when you are going;
   » which city/what cities you are going to visit;
   » what you are going to do once there;
   » how you are feeling now about this trip.

   Write approximately **50 Chinese characters**. (16 marks)

VI. Travel and Tourism

3. Write a diary about your summer camp last June in China. You **must** include the following points:
   » where the summer camp was in China;
   » what you did there;
   » positive and negative aspects of the summer camp;
   » if you wish to recommend this camp to others.
   Write approximately **80 Chinese characters**. Challenge (16 marks)

4. You are writing an article for a Chinese travelling magazine. You **must** include the following points:
   » discuss the usefulness of the guidebooks and/or online travel guides;
   » your best holiday experiences.
   Write approximately **135 Chinese characters**. Challenge (32 marks)

5. You are writing a blog post to promote sports holidays to teenagers. You **must** include the following points:
   » one of your sports holiday experiences;
   » your view on having sports holidays.
   Write approximately **135 Chinese characters**. (Challenge) (32 marks)

[Empty character grid boxes for writing Chinese characters — 4 rows]

6. Translate these sentences into **Chinese**.

(1) She is Chinese. (2 marks)

(2) I went to the city centre with my younger brother. (2 marks)

(3) There are two cats and one fish in my house. (2 marks)

(4) I don't want to be a doctor because doctors are boring. (2 marks)

(5) I went to Italy by train last year. (2 marks)

7. Translate the paragraph into **Chinese.** Challenge

> I am French and I love travelling. I wish to visit China next October. I want to practise my Chinese because I have studied Chinese for 3 years in France. I would also love to learn more about Chinese culture. My father studied in Shanghai 10 years ago and he said there were lots of interesting places and delicious food in China. I think Chinese food will be as good as French food. (12 marks)

_____

_____

_____

_____

_____

_____

VI. Travel and Tourism

VII Lifestyle

 **Listening**

⇢ Lifestyle `Challenge` ⇠

1. Two friends are chatting about the differences in their lifestyle before and after the pandemic took place. Answer the following questions in **English**.

   Person 1
   Example: What was **her** lifestyle like before the pandemic?
   _____Sleep late and no time for sports_____

   (1) How has her/his lifestyle changed? (1 mark)

   (2) What does she intend to do in the future? (1 mark)

   Person 2

   (3) What was **his** lifestyle like before the pandemic? (1 mark)

   (4) How has her/his lifestyle changed? (1 mark)

   (5) What does he intend to do in the future? (1 mark)

✧ Healthy Lifestyle ✧

2. Four people are talking about what they think a healthy lifestyle is. Listen to the recording and complete the sentences in **English** about what each of them thinks.

   Example: Healthy life is to ___eat more healthy food___, and ___eat less fast food___.

   (1) Healthy life is to _____, and _____. (2marks)

   (2) Healthy life is to _____, and _____. (2marks)

   (3) Healthy life is to _____, and _____. (2marks)

 **Speaking**

◆ **Situation-based test**

Topic: Healthy lifestyle `Challenge`

For teachers

» The teacher will start the conversation by greeting and introducing his/her role.
» The teacher can only read out the questions listed below in order and the questions cannot be repeated more than twice.

You are interviewed by a sports magazine about healthy lifestyle.

1	你平常做什么运动？ (two details) Allow the candidate to answer.
2	你认为健康饮食是什么？ Allow the candidate to answer.
3	☺! surprising question 上星期你做了什么运动？ Allow the candidate to answer.
4	你能给十一年级的学生一个保持健康的建议吗？ Allow the candidate to answer.
5	☺? a question Allow the candidate to ask if you have any more questions. *Answer briefly.*

Topic: Healthy lifestyle

For candidates

You are interviewed by a sports magazine about healthy lifestyle.

» Your teacher will start the conversation by greeting you and introducing his/her role.

» You will answer the following five questions in order.

» The question ☺! is an unprepared question.

» The question ☺? is a question you need to ask your teacher.

---

1. Say what sports you normally do. **(two details)**
2. Say what you think is a healthy diet.
3. ☺!
4. Give Year 11 students one suggestion about how to stay healthy.
5. ☺?
   Ask if the reporter has any more questions.

◆ Picture-based test 1

Topic: Social issues

For teachers

» The speaking task should last for **two minutes**.
» The teacher should ask the exact questions listed below in order, and may repeat or paraphrase the questions with similar meaning if needed.

1. 照片里有什么？
2. 在你的国家，不同年龄的人最喜欢的运动是什么？
3. 你认为健康的生活方式是什么样的？
4. 你觉得少吃肉健康吗？为什么？
5. 你参加过什么慈善活动？

Topic: Social issues

For candidates

» Write all your notes on a separate A4 paper.
» Answer the following questions in order.
» You can ask your teacher to repeat questions.
» ☺! means you will answer an unprepared question.

Look at the photo and prepare to answer the following questions in order:

1. Describe the photo;
2. What the most popular sports are in your country for people at different ages;
3. What you think a healthy lifestyle is;
4. ☺!
5. ☺!

VII. Lifestyle

◆ **Picture-based test 2**

Topic: Healthy life for teenager Challenge

For teachers

» The speaking task should last for **three minutes**.
» The teacher should ask the exact questions listed below in order, and may repeat or paraphrase the questions with similar meaning if needed.

1. 照片里有什么？
2. 你认为健康的生活是什么样的？
3. 你参加过什么慈善活动？说一说你参加过的慈善活动。
4. 你觉得现在的青少年有什么健康问题吗？
5. 将来你想从什么方面来提高青少年的健康生活？

Topic: Healthy life for teenager Challenge

For candidates

» Write all your notes on a separate A4 paper.
» Answer the following questions in order.
» You can ask your teacher to repeat questions.
» ☺! means you will answer an unprepared question.

Look at the photo and prepare to answer the following questions in order:

1. Describe the photo;
2. What you think a healthy life is;
3. Have you attended any charity events before? Please describe the events.
4. ☺!
5. ☺!

Two-way discussion questions

Holiday and travels

1. 你喜欢旅行吗？你去过什么国家？你通常怎么去这些国家？为什么？ (4 marks)

2. 旅行的时候，你最喜欢做什么？为什么？ (3 marks)

3. 你上次去旅行是什么时候？和谁一起去的？好玩儿吗？ (3 marks)

4. 那儿的天气怎么样？ (2 marks)

5. 你去过中国吗？你去了哪儿？你觉得怎么样？ (3 marks)

6. 你希望将来能再去中国吗？如果能再去，你希望去哪儿？为什么？ (3 marks)

7. 你今年夏天打算去哪儿度假？为什么？ (2 marks)

❖ Illness ❖

1. Three patients are describing how they feel. Which parts of the body they are talking about and when did the symptoms start? Answer the questions in **English**.

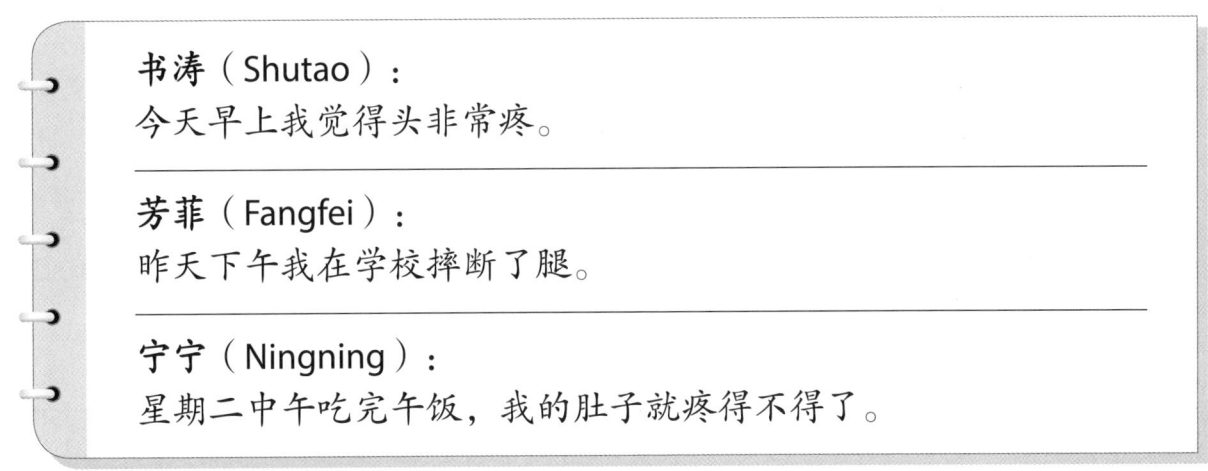

书涛（Shutao）：
今天早上我觉得头非常疼。

芳菲（Fangfei）：
昨天下午我在学校摔断了腿。

宁宁（Ningning）：
星期二中午吃完午饭，我的肚子就疼得不得了。

(1) When did **Shutao** feel unwell? (1 mark)

(2) Which part of **Shutao**'s body was unwell? (1 mark)

(3) When did **Fangfei** feel unwell? (1 mark)

(4) Which part of **Fangfei**'s body was unwell? (1 mark)

(5) When did **Ningning** feel unwell? (1 mark)

(6) Which part of **Ningning**'s body was unwell? (1 mark)

VII. Lifestyle

→ Having a Boyfriend or a Girlfriend (Challenge) ←

2. **Anna** writes an article for the school newspaper about having a boyfriend or a girlfriend during GCSE year. Read the statements below and choose the correct answer for each question. Write the letters in the blanks.

(1) 虽然大人们都认为在中学谈恋爱不好，但是我觉得谈恋爱也有好处。

What does Anna think of the issue? _____ (1 mark)

A	It is not good for secondary school students.
B	It has its advantages.
C	Students should be able to find true love.

(2) GCSE这一年，同学们都觉得压力非常大。我们每天都有考试和很多作业。我们没有时间放松。

What do students think of the GCSE year? _____ (1 mark)

A	They have no time to relax.
B	They are able to balance study and leisure.
C	They think they can deal with the pressure.

(3) 谈恋爱有时候只是为了有一个好朋友和我们聊天儿，让我们不要太担心和紧张。当然，如果两个人可以互相帮助学习，那就更好了。

What is the reason Anna thinks some students have a boyfriend/girlfriend in their GCSE year? _____ (1 mark)

A	They need someone to encourage them.
B	They are trying to find love.
C	They need someone to do their homework with.

 **Writing**

1. You are hosting a mindfulness session for students to learn to deal with stress. Write a notice to the students about the session. You **must** include the following points:
   » when the session will be;
   » where the session will be;
   » how long the session will last;
   » what to bring to the session.

   Write approximately 40 Chinese characters. (16 marks)

2. You write a letter to your Chinese friend about the boot camp you attended last summer. You **must** include the following points:
   » when and where the camp was;
   » why you attended;
   » positive and negative aspects of the boot camp;
   » if you will attend it again or not.

   Write approximately 75 Chinese characters. (16 marks)

3. You are writing an article for a teenage magazine. You **must** include the following points:
   » your typical daily life in GCSE year;
   » your opinion about how school life affects our future.
   Write approximately **125 Chinese characters**. Challenge   (32 marks)

4. Translate these sentences into **Chinese**.

   (1) He likes green vegetables. (2 marks)

   (2) I swam for an hour at the sports centre yesterday. (2 marks)

   (3) I think eating fruit is better than drinking fruit juice. (2 marks)

   (4) Students should play computer games less because it is not good for our eyes. (2 marks)

   (5) I like doing homework whilst listening to music. (2 marks)

5. Translate the paragraph into **Chinese**.

   I am a student in Year 11. Because of the GCSE exams, I have lots of homework and exams every week. Sometimes I am very tired. Although school is stressful, I do love my school life. I have learned a lot, made a lot of friends and have also grown up a lot in the past five years. (12 marks)

VIII Social and Global Issues

🎧 Listening

❖ Local Environment ❖

1. A journalist is interviewing a group of residents in a region about their local environment. What does each resident see as a problem? Write your answers in **English**.

   (1) _____ (1 mark)

   (2) _____ (1 mark)

   (3) _____ (1 mark)

❖ Volunteer Work [Challenge] ❖

2. A group of students are talking about their opinions on doing volunteer work.
   Write **L** if the speaker **likes** the mentioned perspective of the volunteer work,
       D if the speaker **dislike** the mentioned perspective of the volunteer work,
   or **M** if the opinion is **mixed**.

   (1) ☐ (1 mark)

   (2) ☐ (1 mark)

   (3) ☐ (1 mark)

   (4) ☐ (1 mark)

 **Speaking**

◆ Situation-based test

Topic: Voluntary work Challenge

For teachers

» The teacher will start the conversation by greeting and introducing his/her role.
» The teacher can only read out the questions listed below in order and the questions cannot be repeated more than twice.

You are talking to your friend about your experience as a volunteer in the panda reservation centre.

1	你在那儿做了多长时间的义工？ Allow the candidate to answer.
2	你在那儿的工作包括什么？ **(two details)** Allow the candidate to answer.
3	☺! surprising question 那儿的熊猫怎么样？ Allow the candidate to answer.
4	你怎么看做义工这件事情？ Allow the candidate to answer.
5	☺? a question Allow the candidate to ask you what volunteer experience you have had. *Answer briefly.*

VIII. Social and Global Issues

Topic: Voluntary work

For candidates

You are talking to your friend about your experience as a volunteer in the panda reservation centre.

» Your teacher will start the conversation by greeting you and introducing his/her role.
» You will answer the following five questions in order.
» The question ☺! is an unprepared question.
» The question ☺? is a question you need to ask your teacher.

---

1. Say how long you worked there as a volunteer.
2. Say what your daily job included. **(two details)**
3. ☺!
4. Say what your opinion on volunteer experience is.
5. ☺?
   Ask your friend what volunteer experience he/she had.

◆ **Picture-based test 1**

Topic: Protecting our environment `Challenge`

For teachers

» The speaking task should last for **three minutes**.
» The teacher should ask the exact questions listed below in order, and may repeat or paraphrase the questions with similar meaning if needed.

1. 图片里有什么?
2. 你觉得保护森林重要吗?为什么?
3. 你以前参加过环境保护活动吗? **(two details)**
4. 你平常会做一些什么事情来帮助保护环境?
5. 你觉得将来学校还应该做些什么来帮助环境保护?

Topic: Protecting our environment Challenge

For candidates

» Write all your notes on a separate A4 paper.
» Answer the following questions in order.
» You can ask your teacher to repeat questions.
» ☺! means you will answer an unprepared question.

Look at the picture and prepare to answer the following questions in order:

1. Describe the picture;
2. If you think it is important to protect the forests and the reason;
3. If you have attended any environment protection activities before; (**two details**)
4. ☺!
5. ☺!

◆ Picture-based test 2

Topic: Volunteering and future employment Challenge

For teachers

» The speaking task should last for **three minutes**.
» The teacher should ask the exact questions listed below in order, and may repeat or paraphrase the questions with similar meaning if needed.

1. 说说照片里有什么？
2. 你做过志愿者（volunteer）吗？什么时候？
3. 你觉得做志愿者有什么好处和坏处？
4. 你小时候的理想是什么？为什么？
5. 你中学毕业以后打算做什么？为什么？

VIII. Social and Global Issues

Topic: Volunteering and future employment

For candidates

» Write all your notes on a separate A4 paper.
» Answer the following questions in order.
» You can ask your teacher to repeat questions.
» ☺! means you will answer an unprepared question.

Look at the photo and prepare to answer the following questions in order:

1. Describe the photo;
2. Have you done any volunteering work before? When was that?
3. What advantages and disadvantage does volunteering work have?
4. ☺!
5. ☺!

Two-way discussion questions

Topic 1: Society problems

1. 你做过义工吗？什么时候？你做了什么？ *(Nǐ zuòguo yìgōng ma? Shénme shíhou? Nǐ zuòle shénme?)* (3 marks)

2. 你觉得做义工有什么好处？ *(Nǐ juéde zuò yìgōng yǒu shénme hǎochù?)* (2 marks)

3. 你将来会去国外做慈善工作吗？ *(Nǐ jiānglái huì qù guówài zuò císhàn gōngzuò ma?)* (2 marks)

4. 英国街上的乞丐多吗？ *(Yīngguó jiēshang de qǐgài duō ma?)* (1 mark)

5. 你上次帮助他们是什么时候？ *(Nǐ shàng cì bāngzhù tāmen shì shénme shíhou?)* (1 mark)

6. 你有男/女朋友吗？ *(Nǐ yǒu nán/nǚ péngyou ma?)* (1 mark)

7. 你觉得中学生谈恋爱有什么好处和坏处？ *(Nǐ juéde zhōngxuéshēng tán liàn'ài yǒu shénme hǎochù hé huàichù?)* (2 marks)

8. 你吃过中药吗？ *(Nǐ chīguo zhōngyào ma?)* (1 mark)

Topic 2: Environmental problems

9. 英国有哪些环境问题？ *(Yīngguó yǒu nǎxiē huánjìng wèntí?)* (2 marks)

10. 中国环境问题严重吗？ *(Zhōngguó huánjìng wèntí yánzhòng ma?)* (2 marks)

11. 我们应该怎么更好地保护环境？ *(Wǒmen yīnggāi zěnme gèng hǎo de bǎohù huánjìng?)* (2 marks)

12. 你为了保护环境做过什么？ *(Nǐ wèile bǎohù huánjìng zuòguo shénme?)* (2 marks)

13. 为什么环境保护非常重要？ *(Wèi shénme huánjìng bǎohù fēicháng zhòngyào?)* (1 mark)

Topic 3: Unhealthy problems

14. 你觉得现在的人有哪些健康问题？ *(Nǐ juéde xiànzài de rén yǒu nǎxiē jiànkāng wèntí?)* (1 mark)

VIII. Social and Global Issues

15. 我们应该怎么解决这些健康问题？ (2 marks)

16. 为什么有健康的生活习惯非常重要？ (2 marks)

17. 你觉得你以前有什么不好的生活习惯？ (1 mark)

18. 你觉得过健康的生活容易吗？为什么？ (2 marks)

Topic 4: Holiday and travels

19. 你今年有做义工或志愿者的打算吗？ (3 marks)

Topic 5: Health issue

20. 你觉得现在的人有哪些不健康的生活习惯？这些习惯有什么坏处？ (3 marks)

21. 我们应该怎么解决这些健康问题？ (3 marks)

22. 你觉得自己以前有什么不好的生活习惯？ (3 marks)

23. 你觉得你现在的生活习惯怎么样？ (3 marks)

24. 为了生活得更健康，你打算怎么做？ (3 marks)

Topic 6: Environmental issue

25. 中国有哪些环境问题？ (2 marks)

26. 英国的环境问题严重吗？ (2 marks)

27. 为什么环（境）保（护）这么重要？ (2 marks)

28. 你今年还打算为保护环境做些什么？ (3 marks)

 **Reading**

❖ Charity ❖

1. In a charity event, the representatives from different charities are introducing their charities. The table shows what each charity does. Choose the right charity for each statement. Write the letters in the boxes.

A	我们帮助独自住在家中的老年人。
B	我们帮助没有家的人找地方住。
C	我们帮助医院里生病的孩子。
D	我们帮助喝酒的人戒酒。
E	我们帮助小动物。
F	我们帮助保护森林。

(1) Help to save animals. ☐ (1 mark)

(2) Help sick children in hospital. ☐ (1 mark)

(3) Help homeless people. ☐ (1 mark)

(4) Help alcoholics. ☐ (1 mark)

VIII. Social and Global Issues

Environment Challenge

2. **Song Shan** (宋珊) is talking about her family's attitudes towards environmental protection. Read everyone's opinions and choose the correct answer to complete each sentence. Write the letters in the blanks.

   (1) 我爸爸不相信全球变暖，他去哪儿都开车。

   Song Shan's dad _____. (1 mark)

A	drives everywhere
B	thinks global warming has become worse
C	is an environment activist

   (2) 我妈妈每个周末都在我家附近的回收中心做义工。

   Every weekend, **Song Shan**'s mum _____. (1 mark)

A	goes to the city centre to take crafting lessons
B	volunteers in a local recycling centre
C	recycles our daily rubbish in a local recycling centre

   (3) 我哥哥说气候变化会让我们的生活有越来越多的危险。

   Song Shan's elder brother says _____. (1 mark)

A	climate change will bring more danger to our lives
B	the conspiracy about climate change is very dangerous
C	climate change is a fantasy of apocalypticists

   (4) 姐姐很讨厌我，因为我总是说不要买不需要的东西，这会让环境问题更严重。

   Regarding environmental issues, **Song Shan**'s elder sister _____. (1 mark)

A	is really worried
B	is shopping only in local charity shops
C	couldn't care less

3. Read the following news about the global catastrophes around the world. `Challenge`

> 二零二一年，对世界来说是很不容易的一年，气候变暖导致很多灾难发生。七月，德国发大水，很多人死了，房子和汽车被水冲走了。中国郑州下大雨，所以地铁里面有很多水，也有一些人死了。英国也发大水了。七月和八月，土耳其、希腊、意大利和美国都有山火，很多人的家没有了。
>
> 世界上很多地方都出现了极端天气，我们要保护我们的环境，少开车，多坐公共交通或者骑自行车。少用塑料袋，保护森林，节约水和电，多吃青菜，少吃肉或者吃素食。

» 灾难 (zāinàn)：catastrophe

» 郑州 (Zhèngzhōu)：Zhenzhou (capital city of Henan Province)

» 土耳其 (Tǔ'ěrqí)：Turkey

» 极端 (jíduān)：extreme

(1) Choose three correct statements from the options below. Write the letters in the boxes.

☐ ☐ ☐   (3 marks)

A	There were floods in German in June.
B	A city in China flooded, causing water to go into the underground.
C	There were wild mountain fires in the UK.
D	Turkey flooded and lots of house were destroyed.
E	There were wild mountain fires in America.
F	A few countries experienced extreme weather.
G	We should protect the forest.
H	Eating more meat could help us to protect our environment.

(2) According to the news, name any two things we could do to protect our environment apart from protecting the forest according to the news. Answer the questions in **English**.

_____ (2 marks)

VIII. Social and Global Issues

 Writing

1. You are writing on Twitter about environmental protection. You **must** include the following points:
   » different environmental problems;
   » the importance of protecting the environment;
   » your recent involvement in saving the planet;
   » your plan for similar activities in the future.
   Write approximately **110-130 Chinese characters**. **Challenge** (16 marks)

2. You are writing an article for the school newspaper about students doing charity work. You **must** include the following points:
   » the importance of volunteering;
   » your recent experience of helping others.
   Write approximately **120-150 Chinese characters**. Challenge (32 marks)

3. Translate the paragraph into Chinese. **Challenge**

> Many people lost their jobs and houses recently. I think it is because job opportunities are getting less and less but houses are very expensive! I bought some bread and water for the homeless people yesterday and I am going to give them some of my old clothes. **(12 marks)**

IX Education, Future Study and Employment

🎧 Listening

✦ School Life `Challenge` ✦

1. Four secondary school students are talking about their school life.

    Write **L** if the student **likes** the mentioned viewpoint of school life,

    D if the student **dislikes** the mentioned viewpoint of the school life,

    or **M** if the opinion is **mixed**.

    (1) ☐ (1 mark)

    (2) ☐ (1 mark)

    (3) ☐ (1 mark)

    (4) ☐ (1 mark)

✦ School Subjects, Routine and Life Pressure ✦

2. These students are talking about their school life and routines. Answer the questions in **English**.

    (1) Why is he so tired all the time? (1 mark)

    (2) Why does she **rarely have** enough sleep? (1 mark)

IX. Education, Future Study and Employment — 163

(3) What is his favourite school subject? (1 mark)

(4) Why is she and her classmates so worried? (1 mark)

(5) What happened between his friend and him the moment after he refused to show her his homework? (1 mark)

⇢ Future Career Challenge ⇠

3. A girl, **Li Na** (李娜), and a boy, **Wang Long** (王龙), are talking about their ambitions and are analysing them. List **one** good aspect and **one** cause of concern they mention about their career choices. Answer **all** questions in **English**.

Li Na

(1) Good aspect _____ (1 mark)

(2) Cause of concern _____ (1 mark)

Wang Long

(3) Good aspect _____ (1 mark)

(4) Cause of concern _____ (1 mark)

School Life

4. **Xiaoli** (小李) is interviewing **Linlin** (琳琳) about her school. Listen to the recording and choose the answer for each question. Write the letters in the blanks.

   (1) How many lessons does **Linlin** have every day? _____ (1 mark)

A	5
B	6
C	7
D	8

   (2) What time does **Linlin** have lunch? _____ (1 mark)

A	12:00
B	12:20
C	12:30
D	13:00

   (3) What is **NOT** the thing **Linlin** does during break time? _____ (1 mark)

A	Eating
B	Running
C	Reading
D	Chatting

   (4) What would **Linlin** like to do in the future? _____ (1 mark)

A	Be a scientist
B	Be an artist
C	Be an athlete
D	Be a teacher

(5) In addition to the teachers being very good in **Linlin**'s school, what else does **Linlin** like? _____ (1 mark)

A	School facilities
B	School lunches
C	Classmates
D	It's close to home

 **Speaking**

◆ **Situation-based test**

Topic: School

For teachers

» The teacher will start the conversation by greeting and introducing his/her role.
» The teacher can only read out the questions listed below in order and the questions cannot be repeated more than twice.

You are having a chat with a Chinese friend about your current school.

1	你的学校在哪儿？ Allow the candidate to answer.
2	你的学校有什么设施？**(Two details)** Allow the candidate to answer.
3	你最喜欢学什么科目？为什么？**(Two details)** Allow the candidate to answer.
4	☺! surprising question 你觉得你们的校服怎么样？ Allow the candidate to answer.
5	☺? a question Allow the candidate to ask if you like the food in your school's canteen. *Answer briefly.*

IX. Education, Future Study and Employment

Topic: School

For candidates

You are having a chat with a Chinese friend about your current school.

» Your teacher will start the conversation by greeting you and introducing his/her role.
» You will answer the following five questions in order.
» The question ☺! is an unprepared question.
» The question ☺? is a question you need to ask your teacher.

---

1. Say where your current school is.
2. Say what facilities there are in your school. **(two details)**
3. Say what your favourite subject is and why you like it. **(two details)**
4. ☺!
5. ☺?
   Ask if your friend likes his/her school's canteen food.

💬 Two-way discussion questions

My school and future career

Topic 1: My subjects

1. 你们的学校叫什么？有什么设施？ *(Nǐmen de xuéxiào jiào shénme? Yǒu shénme shèshī?)* (2 marks)

2. 你们的学校有多少个学生和老师？ *(Nǐmen de xuéxiào yǒu duōshao gè xuéshēng hé lǎoshī?)* (2 marks)

3. 你最喜欢学的科目是什么？为什么？ *(Nǐ zuì xǐhuan xué de kēmù shì shénme? Wèi shénme?)* (2 marks)

4. 你最喜欢的老师是谁？为什么？ *(Nǐ zuì xǐhuan de lǎoshī shì shéi? Wèi shénme?)* (2 marks)

5. 你会说什么外语？ *(Nǐ huì shuō shénme wàiyǔ?)* (1 mark)

Topic 2: School life

6. 说说你的学校生活。比如，每天早上几点上学？几点放学？中午几点吃午饭？每天上几节课？ *(Shuōshuo nǐ de xuéxiào shēnghuó. Bǐrú, měi tiān zǎoshang jǐ diǎn shàngxué? Jǐ diǎn fàngxué? Zhōngwǔ jǐ diǎn chī wǔfàn? Měi tiān shàng jǐ jié kè?)* (4 marks)

7. 你一般在食堂吃午饭还是自己带饭？为什么？ *(Nǐ yìbān zài shítáng chī wǔfàn háishi zìjǐ dài fàn? Wèi shénme?)* (2 marks)

8. 你参加了学校的什么课外活动？ *(Nǐ cānjiāle xuéxiào de shénme kèwài huódòng?)* (1 mark)

9. 有人说，现在学生的生活太忙、太累了，你觉得呢？ *(Yǒu rén shuō, xiànzài xuéshēng de shēnghuó tài máng, tài lèi le, nǐ juéde ne?)* (2 marks)

10. 你觉得做作业重要吗？ *(Nǐ juéde zuò zuòyè zhòngyào ma?)* (2 marks)

11. 你们的校服是什么样子的？你喜欢穿校服吗？ *(Nǐmen de xiàofú shì shénme yàngzi de? Nǐ xǐhuan chuān xiàofú ma?)* (2 marks)

Topic 3: Future study plan

12. 你中学毕业以后，想去上大学还是去工作？为什么？

(2 marks)

13. 如果你想上大学，上什么大学？你想学什么？为什么？

(2 marks)

14. 你想去国外上大学吗？为什么？ (2 marks)

15. 你以前做过兼职工作吗？什么时候？做了什么？你觉得这个工作经历怎么样？

(2 marks)

16. 你觉得中学生做兼职有什么好处和坏处？ (2 marks)

Topic 4: Future career

17. 你小时候的理想是什么？为什么？ (2 marks)

18. 你现在的理想是什么？为什么？ (2 marks)

19. 你大学毕业以后，有什么打算？ (2 marks)

20. 你以后最想在哪儿工作？在伦敦还是别的地方？为什么？

(2 marks)

Reading

✧ School Subjects [Challenge] ✧

1. Three friends are discussing which extra-curricular session to sign up to. Read the information in the table. Choose the correct option for each person. Write the letters in the boxes.

A	照顾小动物
B	学习心理学
C	学习植物学
D	做木工
E	做饼干

(1) **Xinxin** (心心)'s favourite subject is design and technology? ☐ (1 mark)

(2) **Wanwan** (晚晚) loves to know why people sometimes behave in certain ways. ☐ (1 mark)

(3) **Tiantian** (天天) hopes to become a zoologist in the future. ☐ (1 mark)

✧ School Routine and School Life ✧

2. Five teenagers are talking about their school life on Twitter. Choose the right person for each question and write the first letter of their name in the box.

Write **A** for **Alba**.
Write **B** for **Bella**.
Write **D** for **Danielle**.
Write **K** for **Katy**.
Write **L** for **Leanna**.

Alba	我每天早上七点半走路上学，因为我有中文早课。
Bella	午休的时候，我喜欢和朋友在操场上一边吃三明治，一边聊天儿。
Danielle	上完两节课以后，我们有一刻钟的休息时间。
Katy	下午放学以后，我先去参加网球班，然后才回家。
Leanna	我每天上午有三节课，下午有三节课。

(1) Who has 15 minutes break after two lessons? ☐ (1 mark)

(2) Who enjoys having social time on the playground at lunch time? ☐ (1 mark)

(3) Who has a Mandarin lesson every day? ☐ (1 mark)

(4) Who goes to tennis lessons before returning home? ☐ (1 mark)

✦ Education Post-16 [Challenge] ✦

3. Read the interview done with three students about their plans after graduating from secondary school. Answer the questions in **English**.

一家报纸访问了三个英国中学生。
- 九年级学生：我想先去旅行，因为我想看看这个世界。
- 十年级学生：我打算去找一份兼职工作。我觉得做兼职不但能让我赚一些零花钱，而且将来还能帮助我得到更多的工作机会。
- 十一年级学生：我打算上十二和十三年级，因为我想考大学。我的理想是成为一名生物学家。

(1) Why does the Year 9 student want to travel first? (1 mark)

(2) Why does the Year 11 student plan to continue studying in Year 12 and 13? (1 mark)

(3) What is the aspiration of this Year 11 student? (1 mark)

(4) Name **two** reasons why the Year 10 student plans to look for a part-time job? (2 marks)
①
②

❖ Career and Ambitions Challenge ❖

4. **Bella** writes an article for the school newspaper about young British people's opinions on having work experience and their ambitions for the future. Read each statement and choose the correct answer for each question. Write the letters in the blanks.

(1) 英国的很多年轻人认为社会实践非常重要，因为这能让他们学会怎么和不同的人一起工作。

Why do young people in the UK think having work experience is very important?

_____ (1 mark)

A	To learn how to work with different people.
B	To learn about their colleagues.
C	To learn new things.

(2) 他们认为社会实践能让他们对自己的将来有更清楚的目标，让他们知道自己长大以后能做什么样的工作。

Why do young people like having the work experience? _____ (1 mark)

A	To get some travel experience.
B	To know what kind of person they will be when they grow up.
C	To be more sure about what kind of job they can do after growing up.

IX. Education, Future Study and Employment

(3) 我妈妈说我以后应该当老师，因为当老师虽然压力不小，钱也不多，但是常常跟年轻人在一起能让我总是觉得自己很年轻。

Why does Bella's mother want her to become a teacher? _____ (1 mark)

A	Not too stressful
B	Good money
C	Spending time with young people can make her feel young

(4) 我更想成为一名警察，因为我认为当警察更有意义，我能帮助很多需要帮助的人。

What does Bella want to do in the future? _____ (1 mark)

A	Doctor
B	Policewoman
C	Firefighter

5. Translate this paragraph into **English**. Make sure you write the translation in proper English, **NOT** word to word translation.

> 现在中学生有很多考试，最近就有很多中学生因为学习压力太大生病了。因此，在家的时候，父母一定要多跟孩子聊天儿，给他们做健康的食物，不要总是问他们考得怎么样。

(9 marks)

 **Writing**

1. You are writing to your Chinese pen pal about your school. You **must** include the following points:
   » what time you have your **first and last lesson** every day;
   » positive and negative aspects of your school facilities;
   » the last time you had your favourite lesson and what you liked about it;
   » your future study plan.
   Write approximately **110-130 Chinese characters**. Challenge   (16 marks)

2. You are writing an article for a Chinese e-magazine for young people about holidays. You **must** include the following points:
   » your opinion of school holidays;
   » a memorable holiday you had in the past.
   Write approximately **120-150 Chinese characters**. Challenge   (32 marks)

IX. Education, Future Study and Employment

3. Translate the paragraph into Chinese. **Challenge**

> I walk to school at 7:30 every morning. I study 10 subjects this year but my favourite subject is Maths because it is both useful and easy. I went to visit the Science Museum in the city centre with my classmates yesterday. I want to be a teacher in the future. (12 marks)

X. Old Sayings, Poems and Classic Passages

Mencius

The short passage below is adapted from 《孟子》 by **Mencius** (孟子). Complete the statements by writing **English** words in the blanks.

> 孟子和孔子一样,是有名的教育家。
> 孟子生活在两千多年前的中国。
> 他有很多名言,他曾经说过:"天时不如地利,地利不如人和。"
> 孟子还认为,在团队中最重要的是大家互相帮助,这样才能做成事。

Kǒngzǐ
孔子:Confucius

Example: Mencius was a famous ___educator___ like **Confucius**.

(1) **Mencius** lived in China _____ years ago. (1 mark)

(2) One of his famous saying is, "(When in a battle) the weather is key, but not as important as the _____, however it is the harmony amongst the _____ which counts as the most important factor for victory." (2 marks)

(3) **Mencius** thought that in a team, the most important is the team members _____. Then their team can _____. (2 marks)

Poems

1. Below is an extract from a famous poem 《秋浦歌》 by Li Bai (李白).
   Answer the questions in **English**.
   Line 1: 白发三千丈，
   Line 2: 缘愁似个长。
   Line 3: 不知明镜里，
   Line 4: 何处得秋霜。

   (1) What number is mentioned in **Line 1**? (1 mark)

   (2) How did the author describe the mirror 镜 in **Line 3**? (1 mark)

   (3) Which season is mentioned in **Line 4**? (1 mark)

   (4) On which line is the word for "don't know" used? (1 mark)

2. Below is an extract from a famous poem 《清明》 by Du Mu (杜牧). Answer the questions in **English**.
   Line 1: 清明时节雨纷纷，
   Line 2: 路上行人欲断魂。
   Line 3: 借问酒家何处有？
   Line 4: 牧童遥指杏花村。

   (1) What kind of weather is mentioned in **Line 1**? (1 mark)

(2) Where are the travellers mentioned in **Line 2**? (1 mark)

(3) What kind of restaurant are the travellers asking about in **Line 3**? (1 mark)

(4) What type of village is described in **Line 4**? (1 mark)

3. Below is an extract from a famous poem《无题》by Li Shangyin (李商隐). Answer the questions in **English**.
   Line 1: 相见时难别亦难，
   Line 2: 东风无力百花残。
   Line 3: 春蚕到死丝方尽，
   Line 4: 蜡炬成灰泪始干。

   (1) What word did the author use to describe the feeling of both meeting and leaving loved ones in **Line 1**? (1 mark)

   (2) What direction does the wind come from in **Line 2**? (1 mark)

   (3) What season is mentioned in **Line 3**? (1 mark)

   (4) What has dried up in **Line 4**? _____ (1 mark)

A	River
B	Tears
C	Lake
D	Sea

X. Old Sayings, Poems and Classic Passages

(5) What colour is mentioned in **Line 4**? _____ (1 mark)

A	Red
B	Grey
C	Black

4. Below is an extract from a famous poem 《忆东山二首（其一）》 by Li Bai (李白). Answer the questions in **English**.

   Line 1: 不向东山久，
   Line 2: 蔷薇几度花。
   Line 3: 白云还自散，
   Line 4: 明月落谁家？

   (1) What aspect of nature is mentioned in **Line 1**? (1 mark)

   (2) What colour is used to describe the cloud in **Line 3**? (1 mark)

   (3) What question word is used in **Line 4**? (1 mark)

   (4) On which line are the words "long time" used? (1 mark)

5. Below is an extract from a famous poem 《江雪》 by Liu Zongyuan (柳宗元). Answer the questions in **English**.

   Line 1: 千山鸟飞绝，
   Line 2: 万径人踪灭。
   Line 3: 孤舟蓑笠翁，
   Line 4: 独钓寒江雪。

(1) What two aspects of nature are mentioned in **Line 1**? **(two details)** (2 marks)

(2) What number is involved in **Line 2**? (1 mark)

(3) What transport is used in **Line 3**? (1 mark)

(4) What action is mentioned in **Line 4**? _____ (1 mark)

A	Travelling
B	Playing in the snow
C	Fishing

6. Below is the poem 《马益之邀陈子山应奉秦景荣县尹江上看花二公》 by Yuan Kai (袁凯). Read it and answer the questions in **English**.

   袁凯
   Line 1: 黄家渡西多好春，
   Line 2: 黄家渡上酒能醇。
   Line 3: 看花吃酒唱歌去，
   Line 4: 如此风流有几人。

   (1) Which season does this poem describe? (1 mark)

   (2) **Line 3** describes three activities, name any **two** of them. (2 marks)

   (3) What question word is used in **Line 4**? (1 mark)

X. Old Sayings, Poems and Classic Passages

XI Listening Practice Papers

 **Paper I**

- The exam duration is 45 minutes.
- The mark for each question is shown in brackets. The total marks for this paper is 41.
- You will hear each recording twice.

❖ My Best Friend ❖

1. A boy is talking about his friend. Listen to the recording and choose the right answer for each question. Write the letters in the blanks.

   (1) Which year group is the friend in? _____ (1 mark)

A	10
B	11
C	12

   (2) What does the friend look like? _____ (1 mark)

A	Long hair
B	Black eyes
C	Big ears

❖ Holiday Destination ❖

2. These people are talking about where they went last Christmas. Listen to the recording and find out where each of them went. Write your answers in **English** in the blanks.

   Example: German Christmas market

   (1) Speaker 1: _____ (1 mark)

   (2) Speaker 2: _____ (1 mark)

❖ At School ❖

3. **Meimei** (美美) is talking about her school. Listen to the recording and choose the right answer to complete each statement. Write the letters in the blanks.

   (1) **Meimei** likes her school because _____. (1 mark)

A	she likes the teachers
B	she does lots of sports with friends
C	she has lots of friends in school

   (2) She doesn't like _____. (1 mark)

A	music class
B	math class
C	English class

   (3) The school is close to the _____. (1 mark)

A	sports centre
B	swimming pool
C	shopping centre

❖ Internet ❖

4. **Xiaoyou** (小优) is talking about the Internet. Answer the questions in **English**.

   (1) What does **Xiaoyou** often use to surf the Internet? (1 mark)

   (2) How long does **Xiaoyou** surf Internet every day? (1 mark)

   (3) What does **Xiaoyou** normally do online? (1 mark)

❖ Rubbish Collection Activity ❖

5. **Dahai** (大海) is announcing an activity of rubbish collection. Listen to the recording and choose the correct answer for each question. Write the letters in the blanks.

   (1) **When** is the activity? _____ (1 mark)

A	Monday lunch time
B	Monday afternoon
C	Friday afternoon

   (2) **Where** will the activity be? _____ (1 mark)

A	Streets
B	Seaside
C	Football pitch

❖ Job ❖

6. A lady is talking about her job. Listen to the recording and choose the correct answer for each question. Write the letters in the blanks.

(1) **What** is her job? _____ (1 mark)

A	Chef
B	Teacher
C	Nurse

(2) **How** does she feel about her job? _____ (1 mark)

A	Easy
B	Fun
C	Tiring

❖ Festivals ❖

7. **David** is talking about his first Chinese New Year celebration in China last year. Answer the questions in **English**.

(1) What did he do during the celebration? (1 mark)

(2) What did he not do during the celebration? (1 mark)

(3) What does he wish to get for this coming Chinese New Year? (1 mark)

❖ A Date ❖

8. **Xiaojun** (小军) is calling his girlfriend **Meimei** (美美) about meeting up later. Listen to the recording and choose the correct answer for each question. Write the letters in the blanks.

    (1) What time will they meet up? _____ (1 mark)

A	6:00
B	6:30
C	7:15

    (2) Where will they meet up? _____ (1 mark)

A	The park in front of the library
B	The library to the right of the park
C	The park to the left of the library

    (3) What are they going to do? _____ (1 mark)

A	Watch a film
B	Go shopping
C	Study together

❖ Eating Out ❖

9. Two food critics are talking about the restaurants they went the last night. Complete the following questions in **English**.

    Food critic 1

    Example: What kind of restaurant did **she** go to?

    _____Italian restaurant_____

    (1) What did **she** eat? (1 mark)

(2) What comment did **she** give? (1 mark)

Food critic 2

(3) What kind of restaurant did **he** go to? (1 mark)

(4) What did **he** eat? (1 mark)

(5) What comment did **he** give? (1 mark)

✧ The Legendary Messi ✧

10. **Xiaowei** (小伟) is talking about his idol Messi. Listen to the recording and choose the correct answer for each question. Write the letters in the blanks.

    (1) According to **Xiaowei**, why is Messi leaving Spain? _____ (1 mark)

A	He is retiring.
B	He is too expensive.
C	He is injured.

    (2) When will Messi leave Spain? _____ (1 mark)

A	From the start of this summer
B	After this summer
C	Before this summer

(3) What other hobby does Messi have besides football? _____ (1 mark)

A	Chatting
B	Painting
C	Playing basketball

❖ Green Life ❖

11. **Xincheng** (新成) is talking about what he will do to be environmentally friendly. Listen to the recording and choose **five** correct options from the table below. Write the letters in the boxes.

    He is going to…

    (1) ☐ (1 mark)

    (2) ☐ (1 mark)

    (3) ☐ (1 mark)

    (4) ☐ (1 mark)

    (5) ☐ (1 mark)

A	Cycle to school every day.
B	Turn off lights when leaving a room.
C	Not waste food.
D	Not waste paper.
E	Not buy too many clothes.
F	Use less water.
G	Help with recycling.

Gap Year

12. Yibo (一波) is talking about his plan after the GCSEs. Listen to the recording and choose the correct answer for each question. Write the letters in the blanks.

(1) How long is left before **Yibo** takes his GCSE exams? _____ (1 mark)

A	11 months
B	5 months
C	3 weeks
D	3 months

(2) What does **Yibo** plan to do during the gap year? Choose two answers. _____
(2 marks)

A	Work to make some money
B	Learn about different cultures
C	Be a volunteer
D	Travel around the world

Exchange Programme

13. Tina is an exchange student in China. She is interviewed after watching a show. Listen to the recording. Answer the questions in **English**.

(1) What show did **Tina** watch? (1 mark)

(2) What does **Tina** think of the show? (1 mark)

(3) What activity will **Tina** do tomorrow? (1 mark)

Volunteer Work

14. You hear about a Chinese volunteer opportunity on the radio. Listen to the recording and choose two correct statements. Write the letters in the boxes. ☐ ☐ (2 marks)

A	Volunteers are needed in an old people's home.
B	The volunteer needs to know how to drive.
C	The volunteer needs to accompany old people.
D	The volunteer needs to help do food shopping.

 **Paper II** Challenge

- The exam duration is 45 minutes.
- The mark for each question is shown in brackets. The total marks for this paper is 51.
- You will hear each recording twice.

·> Food <·

1. Two friends are chatting about their eating habits. What did they eat before? What do they eat now? What will they eat in the future? Answer the questions in **English**.

Friend 1

Example: What did **he** like eating before?

　　　　　Roast duck
―――――――――――――――――

(1) What does **he** often eat now? (1 mark)

(2) What is **he** planning to eat more of in the future? (1 mark)

Friend 2

(3) What did **she** eat a lot of before? (1 mark)

(4) What does **she** eat too much of now? (1 mark)

(5) What is **she** planning to eat more of in the future? (1 mark)

XI. Listening Practice Papers

✧ Weather Forecast ✧

2. **Ma Long** (马龙) is talking about the weather from when he was away on holiday last week. Listen to the recording and choose the correct options from the table below. Write the letters in the boxes.

    (1) ☐ (1 mark)

    (2) ☐ (1 mark)

    (3) ☐ (1 mark)

    (4) ☐ (1 mark)

    (5) ☐ (1 mark)

A	A rainy and windy day
B	A sunny day without wind and rain
C	A windy day with a gale force between 7 and 8
D	A cold day with torrential rain
E	A pleasantly cool day
F	A cloudy, overcast day
G	A sunny day with a breeze

✧ Music ✧

3. **Zhou Mei** (周梅) is talking about her love for music. Listen to the recording and choose the correct answer for each question. Write the letters in the blanks.

    (1) What is **Zhou Mei**'s favourite type of music? _____ (1 mark)

A	Country music
B	Pop music
C	Rock music

(2) What is **Zhou Mei** going to do tomorrow? _____ (1 mark)

A	Learn an American country music instrument
B	Go to an American pop music concert
C	Go to an American country music concert

❖ Future Plans ❖

4. A group of students are discussing their future. Listen to the recording and answer the questions in **English**.

   Example: What does this person not want to do in the future?

   _____ Have children _____

   (1) What does this student want to do in the future? (1 mark)

   (2) When does this student plan on going to South Africa? (1 mark)

   (3) What kind of person does this student wish to become? (1 mark)

❖ Marriage/Partnerships ❖

5. You are tuning into Family Radio FM92.5. A programme about relationships is on and different listeners are calling in introducing themselves. Listen to the recordings and choose the correct options from below.

A	Divorced and enjoying the single life.
B	Divorced with children and having a busy life.
C	Newly married but there are problems emerging in the marriage already.
D	Newly married and plans to go on honeymoon soon with her spouse.
E	Has a partner at the moment but not in a hurry to get married.

(1) ☐ (1 mark)

(2) ☐ (1 mark)

(3) ☐ (1 mark)

❖ Holidays ❖

6. **Li Yue** (李月) is talking about her family's discussion on the imminent summer holiday. Listen to the recording and answer the questions in **English**.

    (1) Which city does **Li Yue** want to visit? (1 mark)

    (2) Which city does her younger sister intend to visit? (1 mark)

    (3) Why does her dad want to go to Guilin (桂林)? (1 mark)

❖ Celebrities ❖

7. A group of fashion bloggers are talking about different celebrities whilst watching the broadcast of a recent film festival.

Write **L** if the speaker **likes** the mentioned perspective(s) of the celebrity's dressing style,

D if the speaker **dislikes** the mentioned perspective(s) of the celebrity's dressing style,

or **M** if the opinion is **mixed**.

(1) ☐ (1 mark)

(2) ☐ (1 mark)

(3) ☐ (1 mark)

(4) ☐ (1 mark)

❖ Home Challenge ❖

8. You hear your mum on the phone telling a real estate agent about her ideal house for relocation. Listen to the recording and answer the following questions in **English**.

    (1) What facility must your mum have in this house? (1 mark)

    (2) Why does she want to live in the city centre? (1 mark)

❖ Part-time Jobs Challenge ❖

9. A girl, **Sisi** (思思), and a boy, **Lantian** (蓝田), are talking about their experiences of having part-time jobs. List **one** good aspect and **one** cause of concern they mention about doing part-time jobs. Answer **all** questions in **English**.

    Sisi

    (1) Good Aspect _____ (1 mark)

    (2) Cause of concern _____ (1 mark)

XI. Listening Practice Papers

195

Lantian

(3) Good Aspect _____ (1 mark)

(4) Cause of concern _____ (1 mark)

❖ Environmental Protection ❖

10. An environmentalist is invited to give a speech in your school. Write **three** correct option letters in the boxes on what she said. ☐ ☐ ☐ (3 marks)

A	Turn off the tap when brushing teeth.
B	Avoid excessive buying.
C	Plant more trees in the local park.
D	Recycle used and worn items in the house.
E	Do not waste electricity.
F	Walk more.

❖ Healthy Living ❖

11. The student union of your school is inviting students to give feedback about the quality of the food in the canteen. Listen to the recording and answer the questions in **English**. What does each student see as a problem?

Student A: _____ (1 mark)

Student B: _____ (1 mark)

Student C: _____ (1 mark)

Media

12. What do these people say about their use of different media? Listen to the recording and choose the correct options. Write the letters in the boxes.

Person 1 ☐ ☐ (2 marks)

Person 2 ☐ ☐ (2 marks)

A	I like reading the news on newspapers.
B	I like watching the news on my mobile phone.
C	I think there are too many adverts online.
D	I like posting my latest photos on social media.
E	I hate taking photos.
F	I watched a kung fu film on TV at home yesterday.
G	I went the to cinema to watch a kung fu film yesterday.
H	I hope one day I can become an online stylist.

Advertisement

13. You hear a job advert on the radio. Listen to the recording and choose two correct statements from the options. Write the letters in the boxes. ☐ ☐ (2 marks)

A	They are recruiting a receptionist.
B	They are recruiting a computer engineer.
C	The ideal candidate needs to work on Sundays.
D	The ideal candidate needs to speak fluent Chinese and English.

Social Issues

14. You are listening to the radio of a social correspondent's report followed by a health correspondent. Listen to the recording and choose the right answer for each question. Write the letters in the blanks.

(1) According to the social correspondent, what is the current social problem in the city? _____ (1 mark)

A	Unemployment
B	Housing problem
C	Too many pickpockets

(2) According to the health correspondent, what do the local people suggest will help attract more skilled doctors to work in the countryside? _____ (1 mark)

A	Give them more holidays
B	Give them free houses
C	Give them higher salary

❖ School ❖

15. Yangyang (洋洋), a Year 11 student is talking about his ideal 6th form college. Listen to the recording and choose the correct answer for each question. Write the letters in the blanks.

(1) Where is **Yangyang**'s ideal 6th form college? _____ (1 mark)

A	A college near the water
B	A college in countryside
C	The current school

(2) Why did **Yangyang** choose this college? _____ (1 mark)

A	Less social pressure
B	He loves fish
C	He loves natural landscape

Festivals

16. **Gao Feng** (高峰) and **Luo Hong** (罗红) are talking about festivals and celebrations. Listen to the recording and choose the correct answers from each table. Write the letters in the blanks.

Festivals	
A	Easter
B	the Mid-Autumn Festival
C	Christmas
D	Chinese New Year

Reasons	
A	to have moon cakes
B	to have the family reunion dinner
C	to look for Easter eggs
D	to receive many presents

Which festival does each of them like the most and why?

(1) **Gao Feng** likes _____ because _____ . (2 mark)

(2) **Luo Hong** likes _____ because _____ . (2 mark)

Paper III (Challenge)

- The exam duration is 45 minutes.
- The mark for each question is shown in brackets. The total marks for this paper is 50.
- You will hear each recording twice.

❖ Sports ❖

1. **Xiaoli**（小丽）is talking about her hobbies to her friends. Listen to the recording and complete the sentences by choosing words/phrases from the box. Write the words/phrases in the blanks. You will not need to use all the words in the box.

playing basketball	this year	half an hour	dance show
sports centre	last year	playing football	park
~~supermarket~~	45 minutes	last May	school
swimming	party	an hour	dance competition
playing tennis	school prom		

   Example: **Xiaoli** often goes shopping in the <u>supermarket</u>.

   (1) **Xiaoli** likes running, dancing and _____ . (1 mark)

   (2) **Xiaoli** runs in the _____ . (1 mark)

   (3) **Xiaoli** and her little brother can run up to _____ . (1 mark)

   (4) **Xiaoli** started to learn dancing from _____ . (1 mark)

   (5) Next year, **Xiaoli** would like to participate in _____ . (1 mark)

✧ Living Area ✧

2. **Amy** has recently moved to a new community with her family. She is describing her new living area. Listen to the recording and choose the correct answers. Write the letters in the blanks.

   Example: Amy's new home is ___A___.

A	big
B	small
C	comfortable
D	ugly

   (1) **Amy**'s bedroom is _____. (1 mark)

A	very beautiful
B	very small
C	bigger than her little brother's
D	very big

   (2) **Amy** doesn't have _____ in her bedroom. (1 mark)

A	a bookshelf
B	a computer
C	a bed
D	a table

   (3) **Amy**'s living area has many _____. (1 mark)

A	parks
B	shops
C	schools
D	restaurants

(4) Amy goes to school by _____. (1 mark)

A	car
B	bus
C	cycling
D	walking

❖ My Family and My Friends ❖

3. You are interviewing **Daming** (大明). Listen to the recording and choose three correct statements from the table. Write the letters in the boxes. ☐ ☐ ☐ (3 marks)

A	**Daming** and his family are living in Beijing.
B	**Daming** is in Year 10.
C	**Daming** has two friends in his school.
D	**Daming** likes playing basketball with his friend.
E	**Daming**'s elder sister is in the same school as Daming.
F	**Daming**'s mum is a doctor.
G	**Daming** and his family travel outside London during the weekend.

❖ Holidays ❖

4. **Xiaoshan** (小山), **Wenwen** (文文), **Nana** (娜娜) and **David** (大卫) are talking about their holidays. Listen to the recording and complete the sentences by writing "**really fun**", "**boring**", "**tired**" and "**time wasting**" in the blanks. You can use each opinion more than once.

   (1) **Wenwen** thinks travelling in America is _____. (1 mark)

   (2) **Nana** thinks learning Spanish is _____. (1 mark)

   (3) **David** thinks staying in the mountain area is _____. (1 mark)

   (4) **Xiaoshan** thinks his grandparents' home is _____. (1 mark)

   (5) **Xiaoshan**'s grandparents think their living area is _____. (1 mark)

✧ My School ✧

5. **Mingming** (明明) is describing his school. Listen to the recording and choose the correct option to complete each statement. Write the letters in the blanks.

Example: **Mingming**'s school is in ____B____.

A	Beijing
B	Xi'an
C	Shanghai
D	Guangzhou

(1) **Mingming**'s school is a _____. (1 mark)

A	primary school
B	music school
C	middle school
D	university

(2) **Mingming**'s school does not have a _____. (1 mark)

A	corner shop
B	playground
C	assembly hall
D	library

(3) Next week, **Mingming** will have a _____. (1 mark)

A	English test
B	music test
C	piano performance
D	singing performance

XI. Listening Practice Papers

✦ Environmental Protection ✦

6. You hear this podcast regarding a volunteer recruiting advertisement in your school. Listen to the recording and answer the questions in **English**.

    (1) What is this organisation about? (1 mark)

    (2) If you would like to join this organisation, which floor do you need to go to? (1 mark)

    (3) Please list any **TWO** things you could do if you join this organisation. (2 marks)

    (4) What could you get if you join this organisation? (1 mark)

✦ Using Technology in Daily Life ✦

7. **Dashan** (大山) and **Nana** (娜娜) are talking about how people use technology in their daily life. Listen to the recording and answer the questions in **English**.

    (1) Every day, how many hours does **Dashan** spend using his mobile phone? (1 mark)

    (2) Please list any **TWO** things that **Dashan** uses his mobile phone to do. (2 marks)

    (3) Why does **Nana NOT** like using her mobile phone? (1 mark)

    (4) What does **Nana**'s dad do while he is drinking tea? (1 mark)

✧ Travelling and Ticket Booking ✧

8. **Linlin** (琳琳), **Xiaoming** (小明) and **Li Dong** (李东) are talking about travelling. Listen to the three parts of the recording individually. Choose the correct option to complete each statement. Write the letters in the blanks.

Part A

Example: Linlin traveled to _____C_____ .

A	Xi'an
B	Beijing
C	Shanghai
D	Sanya

(1) Apart from convenience, **Linlin** travelled by underground because it is _____ .

(1 mark)

A	good
B	fast
C	safe
D	cheap

(2) **Linlin** visited _____ .

(1 mark)

A	the zoo
B	the museum
C	the Bird's Nest
D	the Great Wall of China

Part B

(3) **Xiaoming** booked a _____. (1 mark)

A	single room
B	double room
C	shared room
D	family stay

(4) **Xiaoming** will travel in Beijing by _____. (1 mark)

A	underground
B	bus
C	taxi
D	car

Part C

(5) **Li Dong** will travel to Australia because he wants to _____. (1 mark)

A	be a youtuber
B	be a volunteer
C	do a full time job
D	do a part-time job

(6) **Li Dong**'s dad booked a _____ ticket for him. (1 mark)

A	one way flight
B	return flight
C	one way ferry
D	return ferry

Food and Eating Out

9. **Shanshan** (珊珊) is reporting on food culture in China. Listen to the three parts of the recording individually and answer the questions in **English**.

   Part A

   (1) Why does China have lots of different food? (1 mark)

   (2) What do people from northern China like to eat? (1 mark)

   (3) Why can people now cook authentic food? (1 mark)

   (4) What does **Shanshan**'s friend think about cooking now? Give **two** comments. (2 marks)

   Part B

   » 抖音 Dǒuyīn: Tiktok

   (5) What can you do if you find a restaurant that serves very delicious food? (1 mark)

   (6) What can you do if you go to a restaurant made famous by the Internet? (1 mark)

   Part C

   (7) Where can you find bubble tea shops? (1 mark)

   (8) What are the **two** comments made about bubble tea shops that are made famous by the Internet? (2 marks)

Careers

10. **Donglin** (冬林) is talking about his family members' careers. Choose **four** correct statements from the options. Write the letters in the boxes. (4 marks)

Example: | A |

A	~~Donglin's dad is a journalist.~~
B	**Donglin's** dad likes his job because he likes travelling.
C	**Donglin's** mum thinks her job is very fun.
D	**Donglin's** elder brother learns Maths and Physics.
E	**Donglin's** elder brother believes being an engineer is fun and challenging.
F	**Donglin** would like to work part-time.
G	**Donglin** would like to go to Africa in the future.
H	**Donglin's** younger brother would like to work in the post office.
I	**Donglin's** younger brother would like to make lots of money in the future.

XII. Reading Practice Papers

Paper I

- The exam duration is 45 minutes.
- The mark for each question is shown in brackets. The total marks for this paper is 64.

Section A: Reading

❖ Food ❖

1. Some young people are talking about the food they brought for the picnic. Read the statements and choose the correct answer for each person. Write the letters in the blanks.

娜娜（Nana）:
我带了鸡肉三明治和苹果。

大山（Dashan）:
我带了可乐和蛋糕。

大海（Dahai）:
我带了蛋炒饭。

A	chicken noodles
B	apple
C	salad
D	cake
E	egg fried rice
F	dumplings

What did each person bring?

(1) **Nana** brought _____ . (1 mark)

(2) **Dashan** brought _____ . (1 mark)

(3) **Dahai** brought _____ . (1 mark)

❖ Part-time Job ❖

2. **Lili** (丽丽) just started a part-time job. She has written four text messages. Read her messages to complete the statements by writing **English** words/phrases in the blanks.

> 我上星期五开始在咖啡店工作。

> 我每天工作六个小时，一周只工作两天。

> 星期一到星期四我要去学校。我现在在大学学习音乐。

> 除了工作和学习，我也常常去运动中心打网球。

(1) **Lili** started working in a _____ from last Friday. (1 mark)

(2) **Lili** only works _____ days per week. (1 mark)

(3) **Lili** is in university studying _____. (1 mark)

(4) Apart from work and study, **Lili** often goes to sports centre to _____. (1 mark)

✧ Living Environment ✧

3. **Xiaoying** (小英) and **Xiaowen** (小文) are talking about where they live.
   Write **L** if they **like** the aspects mentioned about their local area,
   D if they **dislike** the aspects mentioned about their local area,
   or **M** if the opinions are **mixed**.

> 小英： 我不太喜欢我住的地方，这儿只有楼，没有森林，也没有公园。
>
> 小文： 我家这儿很干净，但是离市中心非常远。不过现在买东西都可以上网，倒也很方便。

Xiaoying

(1) Her opinion of the place she lives. (   ) (1 mark)

(2) Her opinion of the local facilities. (   ) (1 mark)

Xiaowen

(3) Her opinion of the place she lives. (   ) (1 mark)

(4) Her opinion of the local facilities. (   ) (1 mark)

❖ Newly Wedded ❖

4. **Xiaolong** (小龙) is sharing his married life on WeChat. Answer all the questions in **English**.

> 我叫小龙，今年八月刚结婚。我和我的妻子都是医生。去年我们非常忙，但是今年我们终于结婚了！我觉得可能因为我是南方人，我的妻子是北方人，所以我爱吃米饭、我的妻子爱吃面条，但是我们都很爱对方。除了工作，我们每个星期六都会去跑步、爬山，星期天我们会去看我们的爸爸妈妈。

(1) What happened to **Xiaolong** this August? (1 mark)

(2) What are **Xiaolong** and his wife's favourite foods? (**two details**) (2 marks)

(3) What are the reasons for **Xiaolong** and his wife's different eating habits? (**two details**) (2 marks)

(4) What do they do every Saturday? (**two details**) (2 marks)

(5) What do they normally do on Sunday? (1 mark)

❖ Our Teachers ❖

5. Two students are describing their favourite teachers. What are their preferences and reasons? Fill in the blanks in **English**.

> 书涛（Shutao）：
> 我最喜欢我们的科学老师。他虽然很严格，但是非常有趣。
>
> 芳菲（Fangfei）：
> 我最喜欢我们的历史老师。她特别爱笑。

Shutao

(1) His favourite teacher is _____ . (1 mark)

(2) The reasons are _____ . **(two details)** (2 marks)

Fangfei

(3) Her favourite teacher is _____ . (1 mark)

(4) The reasons are _____ . (1 mark)

❖ Poem ❖

6. Below is an extract from a famous poem 《人日思归》 by Xue Daoheng (薛道衡). Answer the questions in **English**.

   Line 1: 入春才七日，
   Line 2: 离家已二年。
   Line 3: 人归落雁后，
   Line 4: 思发在花前。

   (1) Which season is mentioned in **Line 1**? (1 mark)

   (2) Where has the author left for two years in **Line 2**? (1 mark)

(3) Which direction word is used in **Line 3**? (1 mark)

(4) In front of what does the author lose in his thought in **Line 4**? (1 mark)

❖ Healthy Life ❖

7. You are a qualified personal trainer in the community. You are promoting some healthy activities at a school. Read the statements in the table and choose the correct activities to match with the students. Write the letters in the boxes.

A	放学后在公园跑步。
B	周末早上游泳。
C	减少压力的活动。
D	健康饮食咨询。
E	午饭时间乒乓球俱乐部。

Which of the following activities would the students below like to do?

(1) I am very busy during the weekdays. ☐ (1 mark)

(2) I eat lots of junk food. ☐ (1 mark)

(3) I don't like to exercise indoors. ☐ (1 mark)

❖ After the GCSEs ❖

8. A group of friends are talking about their plans after their GCSE exams. Write the first letter of the correct name in the box.

Write **M** for **Meimei**.

Write **T** for **Tiantian**.

Write **Y** for **Youyou**.
Write **L** for **Leilei**.
Write **N** for **Ningning**.

莓莓（Meimei）：
我想去意大利学习意大利语。

甜甜（Tiantian）：
我将来想做甜点师，所以打算去蛋糕店做社会实践。

优优（Youyou）：
我会继续上高中，学习生物。

蕾蕾（Leilei）：
我计划去全世界旅游，先去中国看看。

宁宁（Ningning）：
我想先工作挣一些钱再上学。

(1) Who is going to learn a foreign language? ☐ (1 mark)

(2) Who is going to continue studying? ☐ (1 mark)

(3) Who is going to work before studying? ☐ (1 mark)

❖ Chinese Singing Competition ❖

9. Edward attended a Chinese singing competition. He wrote about it on WeChat. Read his message and choose the correct answer for each question. Write the letters in the blanks.

我今天参加了中文歌唱比赛。因为我中文说得很好，而且唱歌也唱得很好，我的中文老师就让我参加了这个比赛。比赛的时候，我一边唱歌，一边弹吉他。我觉得我唱得很不错。

比赛结束后，老师带我们去她的奶奶家吃饺子。我最喜欢的是牛肉饺子，虽然有点儿辣，但是太好吃了！

(1) Why did Edward's teacher recommend that he should attend the competition? _____ (1 mark)

A	He is a music student.
B	He speaks Mandarin very well.
C	He can write songs himself.

(2) What did Edward do while singing? _____ (1 mark)

A	Play guitar
B	Dance
C	Play martial arts

(3) Where did they go for dumplings after the competition? _____ (1 mark)

A	They went to the teacher's grandma's house.
B	They went to a restaurant.
C	They went to the school canteen.

(4) What dumplings did Edward like the most? _____ (1 mark)

A	Pork dumplings
B	Beef dumplings
C	Fish dumplings

(5) What did Edward think of grandma's dumplings? _____ (1 mark)

A	Over cooked
B	Not very tasty
C	A bit spicy

Internet

10. Five young people are talking about how they use Internet. Write the first letter of the correct name in the box.

Write **L** for **Linlin**.
Write **F** for **Fangfei**.
Write **M** for **Meiling**.
Write **H** for **Haiyan**.
Write **X** for **Xixi**.

琳琳（Linlin）：
我常常上网做作业。

芳菲（Fangfei）：
我开网店卖东西。

美玲（Meiling）：
我一般在网上看新闻。

海燕（Haiyan）：
我经常和朋友、家人在网上聊天儿。

西西（Xixi）：
我的机票都是在网上订的。

(1) Who is doing business online? ☐ (1 mark)

(2) Who often chats with family and friends online? ☐ (1 mark)

(3) Who uses the Internet to do homework? ☐ (1 mark)

→ Viewing a House ←

11. A couple want to view a house advertised on a real estate agency website. Here is an e-mail that they sent to the agency. Read their e-mail and answer the questions in **English**.

> From: tianli.chen@163.com
>
> Subject: 看房
>
> 您好！
> 我和我先生想下个星期来看房子。我们下星期一、星期四和星期五有时间，下午五点以前都可以来。我们想看有三个卧室、有花园、厨房比较大的房子，如果附近有学校就更好了。请问，离房子最近的地铁站在哪儿？
> 等您回邮！谢谢！
>
> 田丽

(1) When is the customer free to view the house? (**two details**) (2 marks)

(2) What type of house would the customer like to view? (**two details**) (2 marks)

(3) What question does the customer ask? (1 mark)

My New School

12. What do these Year 7 students think about their new secondary school?

Write **L** if the student **likes** the mentioned perspective(s) of the new school,

D if the student **dislikes** the mentioned perspective(s) of the new school,

or **M** if the opinion is **mixed**.

(1) 我不太喜欢校服，颜色不好看。 ☐ (1 mark)

(2) 学校四点才放学，时间太长了。 ☐ (1 mark)

(3) 我觉得上学很有意思，但是作业有点儿多。 ☐ (1 mark)

(4) 我在学校交了很多朋友。 ☐ (1 mark)

Folk Story

13. Read this extract from a Chinese folk story. Complete the sentences by writing in **English** in the blanks.

> 有一群朋友一起吃饭，只有一瓶酒。一个朋友说，他们比赛画蛇，谁先画完蛇，谁就喝这瓶酒。
>
> 一个人最先画完蛇，然后他看见别的朋友还没画完，就开始给蛇画脚。可是，在他给蛇画脚的时候，另一个人画完了蛇。另一个人就把酒喝了。
>
> 所以，不要做没有用的事情，这样才能更快成功。

Example: A group of friends met for a meal, but only <u>one bottle of wine</u> was left.

(1) They agreed to draw _____ to compete for the wine. (1 mark)

(2) The first person completing the drawing started to add _____. (1 mark)

(3) The other person completed the drawing when _____. (1 mark)

(4) The story tells us not to do _____ to achieve success quicker. (1 mark)

Section B: Translation

14. Translate this paragraph into **English**. Make sure you write the translation in proper English, **NOT** word to word translation.

去年冬天我和朋友去了德国圣诞市场。那时候天气很冷，还下了雪。我们住在一个小酒店，那里的食物很好吃，人也很友好。我觉得那里的风景比英国漂亮多了。

(9 marks)

Paper II

- The exam duration is 45 minutes.
- The mark for each question is shown in brackets. The total marks for this paper is 61.

Section A: Reading

Poem

1. Below is an extract from a famous poem 《咏柳》 by He Zhizhang (贺知章). Answer the questions in **English**.

   Line 1: 碧玉妆成一树高，
   Line 2: 万条垂下绿丝绦。
   Line 3: 不知细叶谁裁出，
   Line 4: 二月春风似剪刀。

   (1) How is the tree described in **Line 1**? (1 mark)

   (2) What colour is mentioned in **Line 2**? (1 mark)

   (3) What question word is used in **Line 3**? _____ (1 mark)

A	Who
B	What
C	How

   (4) What is the aspect of nature is mentioned in **Line 4**? (1 mark)

Family

2. A family is discussing how to spend the coming weekend. Read the activities in the table. Choose the right option to match with what each person would like to do. Write the letters in the boxes.

A	去饭馆吃饭。
B	在附近的公园捡垃圾。
C	去郊区爬山。
D	在家看电视。
E	去美术馆看展览。

(1) Dad loves keeping fit. ☐ (1 mark)

(2) Mum loves culture. ☐ (1 mark)

(3) Elder sister is an environmental ambassador at her school. ☐ (1 mark)

A Survey

3. Read the survey on where people in England prefer to spend their holiday. Answer the questions in **English**.

> 一家旅游公司采访了住在英国的年轻人、老年人和中年人。
> ・年轻人：非常喜欢去海边旅行，因为可以晒太阳。
> ・老年人：更喜欢去城市旅游，因为城市里有更多博物馆。
> ・中年人：有的喜欢去海边，因为孩子能在大海里学游泳，而且那儿的空气也更新鲜；有的喜欢去城市，他们觉得城市里交通更方便，可以去不同的有名的地方参观。

(1) Why do young people like to have a holiday at seaside? (1 mark)

(2) Why do old people prefer to tour in the city? (1 mark)

(3) What do middle-aged people like to do in the city? (1 mark)

(4) Name **two** reasons why middle-aged people like holidaying at seaside? (2 marks)
　　①
　　②

Work Experience

4. **Bella** did a one-week work experience in a restaurant. Here is her blog on her school website. Choose the correct option for each question. Write the letters in the boxes.

> 上个星期，我在市中心一家意大利饭馆做了一个星期的社会实践。这家饭馆不太大，但是很有名，因为他们自己做的意大利面条好吃得不得了。
>
> 虽然我的工作很简单，但是我觉得非常有用。午饭的时候，厨师教我做意大利面。晚饭的时候最忙，服务员教我怎么帮客人点菜。我最想学怎么做鸡尾酒，但是他们说我现在太小了，不能做酒。

(1) What has **Bella** learnt to do in the restaurant? Choose two answers. ☐ ☐

(2 marks)

A	How to set up the kitchen
B	How to make pizzas
C	How to make pastas
D	How to take the orders
E	How to make cocktails

(2) Which **three** statements are mentioned in the text? ☐ ☐ ☐ (3 marks)

A	This restaurant is located in the city centre.
B	The restaurant specialises in Chinese noodles.
C	The restaurant is not big but it is really famous.
D	Bella is really happy that she learnt how to make cocktails.
E	Although Bella thinks that her work experience is not very useful for her future, it was very interesting.
F	Bella thinks that her job there was easy but very useful.

School Challenge

5. Huang Ping (黄萍) is talking about her new school. Answer the questions in **English**.

> 我的新学校有一个大大的游泳池。我们每个星期有三节游泳课，我觉得太多了！我的老师都特别严格，我每天都有很多作业，但是他们也都非常幽默，他们的课生动极了！我在学校交了很多新朋友，他们又热心又友好，我们每天午饭的时候都坐在一起聊天儿。

(1) What facility in the new school is mentioned by **Huang Ping**? (1 mark)

(2) According to **Huang Ping,** what are the **positive aspects** of the teachers in the new school? **(two details)** (2 marks)

(3) What does **Huang Ping** think of her new friends? **(two details)** (2 marks)

(4) What do they do together every day? (1 mark)

Festivals

6. Five teenagers are talking about festivals and celebrations on Twitter. Read the statement and **tick the correct box** if it is related to that particular person.

Write **B** for **Bella**.
Write **M** for **Madeleine**.
Write **L** for **Lucy**.
Write **F** for **Flip**.
Write **E** for **Ezra**.

XII. Reading Practice Papers — 225

Bella	去年春节，我陪父母去北京看亲戚。我们一起放了鞭炮，还去地坛看了舞狮表演，精彩极了！
Madeleine	我去年和男朋友一起去法国过了圣诞节。我们在圣诞树旁边一边聊天儿，一边送礼物，非常开心！
Lucy	去年中秋节，我和男朋友在上海和我们的笔友见了面。我们吃了月饼，喝了中国绿茶，美味得不得了！
Flip	我和女朋友去年去波兰过了圣诞节。我们一起去了教堂唱圣诞歌，特别有意思！
Ezra	去年端午节的时候，我和我太太一起去了杭州旅行，我们看了精彩的龙舟赛，太棒了！

(1) Who went to see her pen-pal during Mid-Autumn Festival? (1 mark)

B ☐ M ☐ L ☑ F ☐ E ☐

(2) Who watched an exciting dragon boat race? (1 mark)

B ☐ M ☐ L ☐ F ☐ E ☑

(3) Who enjoyed singing Christmas Carols? (1 mark)

B ☐ M ☐ L ☐ F ☑ E ☐

(4) Who set off fire crackers during Chinese New year? (1 mark)

B ☑ M ☐ L ☐ F ☐ E ☐

❖ Celebrity ❖

7. **Qingqing** (青青) has written a letter to **Kangkang** (康康). Read the letter and answer the questions in **English**.

> 康康：
>   你好！我最近非常喜欢一个中国明星，他叫王小博（Wang Xiaobo）。他除了跳舞跳得特别棒以外，还是一个非常好的人，比如最近他的家乡有洪水，他买了很多水和衣服给那些没有了家的人。我认为作为一个名人，不但应该做好自己的工作，而且应该帮助那些需要帮助的人。康康，你最喜欢的名人是谁？
>
>   你的朋友
>   青青

Example: What is the nationality of **Qinging**'s favourite celebrity?

_____Chinese_____

(1) What does this celebrity **Wang Xiaobo** specialise in? (1 mark)

(2) What has **Wang Xiaobo** done to help the victims of the flooding? (1 mark)

(3) In **Qinging**'s opinion, what should famous people do apart from doing their jobs well?

(1 mark)

❖ Technology ❖

8. Sophie writes an article for the school newspaper about young people and the use of their mobile phones. Read their statements and choose the right answer for each question. Write the letters in the blanks.

(1) 现在大部分的英国年轻人已经很少在电视机上看电视了。

How many young people in Britain nowadays are still watch TV using a TV set? _____

(1 mark)

A	A few of them
B	Most of them
C	None of them

(2) 他们觉得在手机上看电视、看电影更方便，因为他们可以在任何地方看他们想看的节目，比如在公车上、火车上或者走路的时候。

Why do they think that watching TV on a mobile phone is more convenient? _____

(1 mark)

A	They can watch their favourite programmes wherever they are.
B	They can record their favourite programmes wherever they are.
C	They can stop the programme whenever they need to.

(3) 不过，玩手机真的太容易上瘾了！

What worries Sophie expresses about using a mobile phone? _____

(1 mark)

A	It is too dangerous!
B	It is too expensive!
C	It is too addictive!

(4) 因为手机上有各种各样的游戏和社交媒体，不会让你无聊。

Why does she say so? _____ (1 mark)

A	There is a wide range of newsreels about our society to keep you informed.
B	There is a wide range of simulated platforms such as swimming games, without you actually getting soaked.
C	There is a wide range of games and social media to keep you entertained.

Lao Tzu

9. The extract below is adapted from the 《道德经》 by **Lao Tzu** (老子). Complete the sentences in **English** by writing in the blanks.

> 老子是中国最有名的思想家和史学家之一。
> 他曾被列为世界文化名人。
> 他有很多名言，曾经说过："知者不言，言者不知。"
> 老子认为真正聪明的人不会总是告诉别人自己聪明。
> 这样，我们能成为更好的人。

» 思想家 (sīxiǎngjiā)：thinker

Example: Lao Tzu was one of the most famous thinkers and ___historians___.

(1) He was once selected to be a _____ celebrity. (1 mark)

(2) One of his famous saying is, "People who really know it all rather keep silent, those who talk nonstop actually _____". (1 mark)

(3) **Lao Tzu** thought that genuinely smart people _____. (1 mark)

(4) Then we can _____. (1 mark)

Healthy Living

10. Zhang Hai (张海) is talking about his family's eating and living habits. Read each statement and choose the correct option to complete each sentence. Write the letters in the blanks.

(1) 我爸爸每天都要抽一包烟，所以他常常嗓子不舒服。

Every day, **Zhang Hai**'s dad would _____. (1 mark)

A	eat a whole loaf of bread
B	make dumplings
C	smoke a whole pack of cigarettes

XII. Reading Practice Papers

(2) 我妈妈总是说，每天早上起床后喝一杯蔬菜汁能让你更健康。

Zhang Hai's mum thinks by doing what can we become healthier? _____ (1 mark)

A	Drinking a glass of veg juice after getting up in the morning
B	Drinking a glass of fruit juice after getting up in the morning
C	Drinking a cup of veg soup after dinner before going to bed

(3) 我以前最喜欢吃快餐，但是现在我更喜欢自己做饭吃。

Zhang Hai prefers _____ now. (1 mark)

A	to eat fast food
B	to cook for himself
C	to eat what his mum cooks

(4) 我姐姐最近有点儿超重，因为她吃太多甜的东西了。

What health problem is **Zhang Hai**'s elder sister facing at the moment? _____

(1 mark)

A	She is a little overweight.
B	She is a little underweight.
C	She has a few problems with her teeth.

❖ Charity Work ❖

11. **Dashan** (大山) has written a letter to **Xiaoyu** (小雨) about charity and volunteer work. Read the letter and answer the questions in **English**.

> 小雨：
> 　　你好！很久没联系了，你最近怎么样？
> 　　最近因为疫情问题，伦敦失业的人越来越多。昨天，我和中文班的同学一起去我家附近的超市买了很多食物给街上的乞丐。下个周末，我们还打算去老人院为老人们做晚饭、打扫房间。小雨，你做过志愿者或者义工吗？
>
> 　　　　　　　　　　　　　　　　　你的朋友
> 　　　　　　　　　　　　　　　　　大山

(1) According to **Dashan**, what happened in London recently? (1 mark)

(2) What did **Dashan** and his classmates do to help with the phenomenon? (1 mark)

(3) At the end of the letter, what is **Dashan**'s question to **Xiaoyu**? (1 mark)

(4) What does **Dashan** plan to do in the care home next weekend? Name **two** details.

(2 marks)

⟡ Environmental Issues ⟡

12. People are expressing their concerns and opinions to the local leaders of their respective living areas.

> 安健（Anjian）：
> 　　我以前常常去我家附近的河边钓鱼，但是现在几乎看不到鱼了。河水越来越脏，里面还有很多垃圾，这也给附近人们的健康带来了严重的影响。我希望你能让附近的工厂不要把工业脏水倒进河里了。
>
> ---
>
> 子文（Ziwen）：
> 　　我很久没去我家附近的树林散步了，因为那里的树越来越少、房子越来越多。这不但让空气越来越不新鲜，而且气候变化问题也严重了。您能不能让房地产商人们停止砍树？如果树林都变成了住房，那下大雨的时候雨水去哪儿呢？

Who do the following statements apply to?
Tick **A** if the statement applies to **Anjian**.

Tick **Z** if the statement applies to **Ziwen**.
Tick **both of the boxes** if the statement applies to both **Anjian** and **Ziwen**.

(1) There is severe deforestation in my local area. (1 mark)

A ☐   Z ☐

(2) I used to do outdoor activities often. (1 mark)

A ☐   Z ☐

(3) I am worried about the danger of flooding. (1 mark)

A ☐   Z ☐

(4) Local people's health is really impacted by the pollution. (1 mark)

A ☐   Z ☐

(5) I want the local government to stop the factories releasing industrial waste water into the river. (1 mark)

A ☐   Z ☐

Section B: Translation

13. Translate this paragraph into **English**. Make sure you write the translation in proper English, **NOT** word to word translation.

> 我今年二十五岁，在大学里学物理。昨天，我去伦敦南部参观了科学博物馆，在那儿我看到了很多有意思的东西。我下个周末打算去市中心看电动汽车展。如果你也感兴趣，就跟我一起去吧！

(9 marks)

Paper III Challenge

- The exam duration is 45 minutes.
- The mark for each question is shown in brackets. The total marks for this paper is 50.

Section A: Reading

1. **Xiaoli** (小丽) studys in a boarding school. She is looking at her school menu for next week. Read the menu and answer the questions in **English**.

   友爱中学菜单

   早饭
   - 星期一到星期五：粥、牛奶、包子、面包、鸡蛋、鸡肉、苹果

   午饭
   - 星期一到星期五：米饭、面条、牛肉、鸡肉、青菜、西红柿炒鸡蛋、汤、苹果、香蕉、茶、果汁
   - 星期五还有：比萨、鱼、薯条、汉堡包、可乐、三明治
   （星期五的午饭健康食物免费，不健康的食物收费九元）

   晚饭
   - 星期一到星期五：饺子、猪肉、鸡肉、蛋炒饭、青菜、各种水果

   (1) For which meal can **Xiaoli** eat tomatoes fried with eggs? (1 mark)

   (2) For Friday lunch, how much does it cost if **Xiaoli** eats pizza? (1 mark)

   (3) For which meal can **Xiaoli** eat watermelon? (1 mark)

2. Read the passage below and choose the correct answer for each question. Write the letters in the blanks.

小山（Xiaoshan）每天都用电脑，因为他每天要上网学习、做作业，他也会在网上听音乐、聊天儿。有时候，小山还要发电子邮件。

小山的爸爸妈妈有时候用电脑，他们喜欢看电视，可是小山觉得看电视很无聊。

小山的爷爷奶奶不用电脑，他们有时候用手机打电话给朋友。他们不会用电脑，但是小山的爷爷很想学习电脑，他想在网上买东西。

(1) How often does **Xiaoshan** use computers? _____ (1 mark)

A	Occasionally
B	Sometimes
C	Often
D	Every day

(2) Which one is **NOT** why **Xiaoshan** uses computer? _____ (1 mark)

A	Playing computer games
B	Doing homework
C	Chatting online
D	Sending emails

(3) What does **Xiaoshan** think of watching TV? _____ (1 mark)

A	Fun
B	Boring
C	Waste of time
D	Bad for the eyes

(4) How do **Xiaoshan**'s grandparents communicate with their friends? _____

(1 mark)

A	Meet friends
B	Call friends
C	Write letters to friends
D	Email friends

(5) Why would **Xiaoshan**'s grandfather like to learn how to use a computer? _____

(1 mark)

A	Play online games with Xiaoshan
B	Search information
C	Shop online
D	Make free online calls

3. Read the passage below and answer the questions in **English**.

明明（Mingming）今年十六岁了，他以前很喜欢学习，但是不喜欢运动，他经常生病。后来，他的医生让他多运动，多吃健康的食物，比如青菜和鸡肉。他开始每天跑步，偶尔游泳，他的身体越来越好。现在他经常和他的朋友一起运动。他喜欢各种各样的运动，尤其是户外运动，比如打网球和打篮球，等等。

(1) What did **Mingming** like before? (1 mark)

(2) Why did **Mingming** often get sick before? (1 mark)

(3) What are the **two** suggestions the doctor gave to **Mingming**? (2 marks)

XII. Reading Practice Papers

4. Read the information below and choose the correct name among **Xiaoshan** (小山), **Daming** (大明), **Yitian** (一田) and **Shanshan** (珊珊) to complete the statements. You may need to write each name more than once.

```
小山  • 上九年级
      • 会说汉语和英语
      • 去过法国，明年很想去英国
      • 很喜欢中国节日

大明  • 在大学学习历史
      • 去过长城
      • 最喜欢吃牛肉面

一田  • 有一个妹妹
      • 爱好是跑步和打篮球
      • 喜欢参观博物馆

珊珊  • 中国人，会说汉语、英语、西班牙语和意大利语
      • 在中国上过学，现在在英国上中学
      • 将来想做一个医生
```

Example: ___Xiaoshan___ is in Year 9.

(1) _____ is interested in Chinese New Year. (1 mark)

(2) If you would like to visit the Great Wall of China, you should ask _____ as your tour guide. (1 mark)

(3) _____ would like to be a doctor in the future. (1 mark)

(4) _____ is in the UK now. (1 mark)

(5) If you visit a museum, you should go with _____. (1 mark)

5. The passage below is from **Ding Yi**'s (丁一) blog. Answer the questions in **English**.

> 我的学校在市中心，学校里有很多教室。今年我有六门课，我要学习数学、科学、历史、生物、音乐和体育。
>
> 明年我要参加高考，我想上大学，以后做一个演员。我觉得做演员非常有意思，我可以过别人的生活，也可以赚很多钱。
>
> 我的弟弟跟我在一个学校，他今年上十年级。他数学学得很好，但是他的历史不太好，有时候我会帮助他学习历史。我的弟弟将来想做一个数学老师，因为他喜欢孩子。

(1) Where is **Ding Yi**'s school? (1 mark)

(2) Next year, what will **Ding Yi** participate in? (1 mark)

(3) What job would **Ding Yi** like to do in the future? (1 mark)

(4) Which subject is **Ding Yi**'s younger brother good at? (1 mark)

(5) What job would **Ding Yi**'s younger brother like to do in the future? (1 mark)

6. The passage below is from **Ningning**'s (宁宁) blog. Choose the correct answer for each question. Write the letters in the blanks.

> 世界很大，你想去看看吗？
>
> 二零一五年，有一个老师叫顾少强，她说："世界很大，我想去看看。"我觉得去旅行非常酷，我希望我也能去世界上的很多国家看看。
>
> 我去过欧洲的很多地方，比如英国、法国、意大利、西班牙。我也见到过很多有意思的人，吃过很多好吃的，比如去英国的时候，我吃了鱼和薯条，鱼很好吃，薯条一般；去意大利的时候，我吃了意大利面，我非常喜欢，因为中国也有很多面条。去旅行的时候，我还参观了博物馆，我喜欢看每个国家的历史。
>
> 将来，我想去亚洲和非洲的很多国家玩。我想认识很多朋友，也想看看我没见过的东西。

Example: When did the teacher mention that she would like to travel around the world?

_____A_____

A	In 2015
B	In 2016
C	In 2017
D	In 2018

(1) What does **Ningning** think about travelling? _____ (1 mark)

A	Very boring
B	Very fun
C	Very cool
D	Very cheap

(2) Most countries that **Ningning** has been to are in which continent? _____

(1 mark)

A	America
B	Africa
C	Asia
D	Europe

(3) What did **Ningning** do when she travelled to other countries? Choose **two** options. _____

(2 marks)

A	Met lots of fun people
B	Made lots of good friends
C	Ate lots of delicious food
D	Saw lots of new things

(4) Where did **Ningning** also like to visit when she travelled? _____

(1 mark)

A	Libraries
B	Museums
C	Art galleries
D	Theatres

7. Four students are describing their living areas. Read their descriptions and complete the two tasks below.

东东（Dongdong）：我住在农村，我住的地方不仅漂亮，而且很安静。我家旁边有一个火车站，去市中心很方便。我和我的妹妹每天做完作业就会去散步。

小山（Xiaoshan）：我家在大城市。城市里有很多人，很吵，环境也不太好，我家附近常常有垃圾。我家不远有大公园、运动中心和百货商场，我去运动非常方便。

大明（Daming）：我以前住在山区，那是一个很小的地方，只有一个学校和一个商店。如果我要买很多东西，我要去很远的地方。但是我喜欢这个地方，因为山区的每个孩子都是我的朋友。

张一（Zhang Yi）：三年前，我开始住在我的新家，我的家在海边。每年有很多人来海边旅行。海边有很多纪念品商店，但是没有很多工作机会。明年我想要去大城市工作。

Complete the sentences by writing their names, **Dongdong**, **Xiaoshan**, **Daming** or **Zhang Yi**.

Example: ___Xiaoshan___ lives in a big city.

(1) _____ has many friends. (1 mark)

(2) _____ would like to move in order to find a job. (1 mark)

(3) _____ is not satisfied with the living area. (1 mark)

(4) _____ has easy access to the town centre. (1 mark)

Answer the following questions in **English**.

(5) How does **Xiaoshan** describe his living area? (1 mark)

(6) What does **Zhang Yi** have in his living area? (1 mark)

8. Read the passage from **Tiantian**'s blog below. Answer the questions in **English**.

我的二零二零和二零二二

我是中国人，现在是一个留学生，在英国的一个大学学习英语。

二零二零年是非常困难的一年，全世界都有疫情。很多人生病了，但是不能去医院，因为医院没有地方。人们不能去工作了，学生也不能去学校了。我每天都在网上上课，我也只能在网上见我的朋友。很多商店和饭店都关门了，很多人没有工作了。人们也不能去国外旅行了，因为飞机很少。我想回中国，但是买不到机票。

今年是二零二二年，生活慢慢变好了，我可以在公园和朋友见面，也可以去学校学习。饭店开门了，商店也开门了，昨天我去了伦敦市中心，看见了很多人，我非常高兴。我知道疫情还没结束，还需要很长时间，但是会越来越好的。

» 疫情 (yìqíng)：pandemic

(1) Why could lots of people not go to the hospital when they were sick? (1 mark)

(2) Name any **two** places people **could not** go in 2020. (2 marks)

(3) Why people could not travel abroad? (1 mark)

(4) Name **one** of the things that **Tiantian** can do this year. (1 mark)

9. Read the world news below. Complete the two tasks below.

英国新闻：因为疫情，2020年的欧洲杯在2021年举行。英格兰的足球队非常年轻，但是他们踢得非常好，一直踢到进入决赛。决赛是在伦敦举行的，英格兰对意大利，有很多人看了比赛，但是很遗憾，英格兰足球队输给了意大利足球队。人们说："没关系，下次欧洲杯的时候，英格兰足球队会非常有经验。"

中国新闻：今天，东京奥运会结束了，很多国家的运动员都取得了很好的成绩：中国有三十八块金牌，美国有三十九块金牌，英国也有二十二块金牌，日本的金牌比英国的多。中国队在乒乓球、体操、羽毛球、跳水、射击、举重等方面都有很好的成绩。英国自行车运动员比赛一直很好，这次奥运会得到了金牌。这次奥运会还有一个最小的运动员布朗（Brown），她十三岁，她参加了公园滑板，获得了铜牌。美国的游泳和跑步都取得了非常好的成绩。

(1) What does this news tell us? Choose **three** correct statements from the table and write the letters in the boxes. ☐ ☐ ☐ (3 marks)

A	The England football team is very young.
B	Football fans felt very upset after England lost the European Cup final.
C	China won 38 medals in total.
D	The UK won more gold medals than Japan.
E	China is very good at ping-pong and gymnastics.
F	The UK cycling team started to be the world top team a few years ago.
G	Sky Brown won a silver medal.
H	Sky Brown is the youngest Olympic athlete so far.

Answer the following questions in **English**.

(1) What do people think about the England football team when they play the next European Cup? (1 mark)

(2) Name one of the sports that America did really well in. (1 mark)

Section B: Translation

10. Translate this paragraph into **English**. Make sure you write the translation in proper English, **NOT** word to word translation.

> 我的爸爸有一个体育商店,卖运动的衣服和鞋,等等。我的爸爸喜欢他的商店,因为他非常喜欢运动,他希望告诉人们运动的时候应该穿什么。以前他要做广告,现在不用了,因为越来越多的人开始运动,人们知道运动可以让自己很健康。

(7 marks)

Transcript

I. Me, My Family and My Friends

1. Family and Personalities

Example：我爸爸又高又帅。
（1）我妈妈有大大的、蓝色的眼睛。
（2）当我有需要的时候，姐姐总是帮助我。
（3）我弟弟长得很可爱，但是他真的很烦人。

2. My Family

我的爸爸是一个工程师，他每天都有很多工作。我妈妈是家庭主妇，她常常很忙。我姐姐比我大两岁，她是大学生。

3. Describing People and Personalities

马丽是中国人，她会说汉语、英语和法语。她不高也不矮，很漂亮。她非常喜欢户外运动。小田是一个中学生，他很高，喜欢打篮球，也喜欢看电影。他想做一个演员。大明是一个有趣的人，他有点儿胖，因为他不喜欢运动，还喜欢吃不健康的食物。

4. Marriage and Relationships

Person 1

以前，我想有一个盛大的婚礼；现在，我觉得自己一个人挺好的；以后，我不想要孩子。

Person 2

小时候，我觉得单身更自由，但是现在我结婚了，以后我打算要两个孩子。

5. Mr Wang and His Family

王先生和王太太有一个儿子和一个女儿。他们的儿子在大学学习，他们的女儿是一个中学生，她喜欢跳舞。

他们一家人的关系非常好，常常一起去旅行。去年十二月，他们订了火车票去法国滑雪。王先生的儿子滑雪滑得非常好，但是他的女儿不太喜欢滑雪。明年，他们还想一起坐飞机去非洲玩。

II. Free Time Activities

1. Food

马田：小英，你喜欢吃什么？
小英：我喜欢吃青菜，也喜欢吃鸡肉，因为青菜和鸡肉都很健康。
马田：小美，你呢？
小美：我喜欢吃快餐，因为快餐很方便，我每星期日都吃快餐。马田，你喜欢吃什么？
马田：我是西班牙人，我喜欢吃西班牙菜。我妈妈会做西班牙菜、法国菜、日本菜和中国菜。

2. Sports

我十五岁。我很喜欢运动，因为运动很健康。每星期一，我和我的朋友在学校游泳，我们游半个小时的泳。我也喜欢和我的弟弟一起踢足球，我踢得很好，我弟弟踢得不太好，但是他打篮球打得比我好。我爸爸妈妈都喜欢打网球，他们周末去打网球，但是我不喜欢打网球。我妈妈还喜欢跑步。

3. Music

大林：小美，你周末想做什么？
小美：星期六我要去听音乐会。你呢？
大林：我星期日有一个表演，我要唱歌。
小美：唱什么歌？
大林：唱一首中国歌。我的朋友要表演一个跳舞的节目。
小美：太好了，我要去看。
大林：好。下个月我要去中国音乐节，你想和我一起去吗？
小美：好，我和你一起去中国音乐节。

4. Eating Out

记者：方方，你是哪国人？
方方：我是英国人。我来北京看我的朋友。
记者：欢迎来北京。你今天想吃什么？
方方：我第一次来北京，我的朋友告诉我北京烤鸭很好吃，所以我今天来吃北京烤鸭。
记者：你在北京吃了什么？
方方：我吃了蛋炒饭、羊肉，还有饺子。
记者：什么中国菜最好吃？
方方：我最喜欢吃辣的，因为在英国我不吃辣的。

记者：你还想在北京吃什么？
方方：我觉得我还想吃牛肉。但是我明天就要回英国了，明天早上，我只能吃快餐了。
记者：希望你喜欢中国菜。

5. TV

Friend 1：小时候我最喜欢看动画片，现在我总是看体育比赛，将来我想多看科学节目。
Friend 2：以前我喜欢看做饭的节目，但是现在我常常看流行音乐会，以后我打算多看旅游节目。

6. Celebrities

（1）今年，中国有很多新演员，而且他们的表演都太棒了！
（2）拍功夫电影很赚钱，就是太危险了。演员很容易受伤、生病。
（3）越来越多的人在网上看电影，不去电影院了，我很担心我们的将来。
（4）拍历史电影又有意思又有意义，可惜没有人会给你钱。

III. Technology in Everyday Life

1. The Internet

（1）记　者：你常常上网吗？
　　　男学生：我很喜欢上网，每天上三个小时网。
（2）记　者：你觉得上网怎么样？
　　　女学生：我觉得上网可以帮助学习。
（3）记　者：你一般上网做什么？
　　　男学生：我一般上网看电影。

2. Technology

我住在北京，我的儿子住在伦敦。以前，我不会上网，所以我们常常打电话，但是电话费太贵了。现在我们上网打电话，我也会写电子邮件、发短信了。今年，我的孙子从英国来中国上大学。他和他的爸爸也常常用微信打电话。我觉得科技太好了，不但方便，而且便宜。

3. Social Media

（1）我叫子欣。我是学生。我没有手机，也没有电脑，所以我不用社交媒体，但是我很想知道社交媒体是什么样的。

（2）我叫小白。我天天用社交媒体聊天儿，交朋友。我有一个网上的小店，我需要用社交媒体来做生意。

（3）我叫婷婷，我觉得社交媒体对年轻人太不好了。年轻人应该少用社交媒体，多读书。

（4）我叫美玲，我在国外学习。社交媒体是我和父母朋友聊天儿的地方。我想家的时候和学习压力大的时候，社交媒体给了我很大的帮助。

IV. Customs and Festivals

Festivals

春节是中国的新年，我最喜欢春节，因为春节是中国最重要的节日。大年三十晚上，一家人要在一起吃饭。那天会有很多好吃的：饺子、鸡肉、鱼，等等。春节的时候，人们不工作，一般要放假七天。人们会放鞭炮，看舞龙和舞狮，也会看电视节目，还要去亲戚朋友家拜年，很热闹。

V. Where You Live

1. At the Tube Station

（1）兰兰：你好，请问公园在哪儿？
工作人员：你看，公园就在地铁前边。

（2）兰兰：谢谢你！请问学校怎么走？
工作人员：学校在公园的左边，坐公共汽车五分钟。

2. My Community

（1）燕燕：我叫燕燕，我住的地方有很多设施，非常方便，学校、火车站、商店都有，但是人很多，也很吵。

（2）罗俊：我叫罗俊，我住的地方十分安静，也很安全，可是有点儿无聊。

3. Around My Living Area

我住在北京市中心。我家附近很干净，也很方便，有一个大超市、一个大公园、一个银行和一个百货商场。我常常在公园里跑步。周末，我和家人一起去超市买东西。我家离我的学校很近，走路十分钟。

4. House

我的家很大，有三个卧室、一个客厅、一个厨房、一个厕所和一个书房，还有一个很漂亮的花园。我爸爸妈妈的卧室比我的卧室大，我的卧室比我妹妹的卧室大。我的爸爸喜欢在书房工作，我每天晚上在客厅做作业。每周末上午，我和我的家人在花园里一边喝茶一边看书。我很喜欢我的家。

5. Go Shopping

我家旁边有一个很大的百货商场，一楼是超市，二楼卖文具，三楼卖衣服，四楼卖手机和电脑。每个周末，我和我的家人都会去百货商场。我的爸爸妈妈去超市买牛奶、面包、牛肉和其他好吃的，我和弟弟喜欢去二楼买文具。有时候爸爸和妈妈会去三楼给我和弟弟买衣服。下个星期，我就十五岁了，我的爸爸妈妈要给我买一个手机，所以我们要去四楼。

6. Shopping

（1）我叫大明，我经常去文具店买文具。文具店在我的学校旁边，我去买笔又方便、又便宜。昨天，我和我的朋友去买了两个本子和一个橡皮，一共15块钱。

（2）我叫小丽，我喜欢在网上买衣服，因为在网上我可以看到很多衣服。我可以用我妈妈的信用卡付钱。衣服很快就能送到我家，非常方便。

（3）我叫马田，我常常去我家附近的超市买吃的，因为超市的青菜和水果很新鲜。去超市买东西的时候，我可以走路，这对我的健康也很好。

（4）我叫美美。上个月，我在网上买了一个电脑。我觉得在网上买电脑很容易，只花了半个小时。昨天，我买的电脑到了，我非常喜欢它。

7. Daily Routine

Part A

小林：大卫，你在英国，可以说说你学校的时间表吗？

大卫：当然可以。我每天七点起床，八点骑自行车去学校。我上午有四节课，第一节课八点半开始。我十二点半在食堂吃午饭。我下午有两节课，三点半放学回家。

小林：你放学很早。你学校有什么课？

大卫：我上九年级。我有数学课、科学课、汉语课、音乐课、体育课，等等。我一共有十门课。

小林：你最喜欢什么课？

大卫：我最喜欢汉语课，因为我的汉语老师很有意思，而且以后我想去中国工作，所以我要好好学习汉语。

Part B

小林：珊珊，你现在在中国，可以说说你的日常生活吗？

珊珊：好。我今年十七岁，我在学校有六个科目。

小林：你每天几点去学校？

珊珊：我每天七点半去学校，下午五点放学。

小林：中国的上学时间很长啊。

珊珊：是的。明年我要去大学学习了，所以现在我要好好学习。每天放学以后，我和我的朋友会一起去游泳，因为游泳非常健康。

小林：你有作业吗？

珊珊：我有很多作业，有时候我做作业要做三个小时。

VI. Travel and Tourism

1. Weather Forecast

明天高温，温度在35度左右。下午三

点以后有大雨，请带好雨伞。

2. Hotel

我住在山区，空气新鲜还非常安静。

3. Fangfei's Stay

我住在湖边，这里很不错，就是晚上有点儿冷。

4. Holidays

去年八月，我和爸爸妈妈一起去了法国。法国离英国不远，我们坐了三个半小时的船去法国。我们很喜欢坐船，因为可以看到大海。大海又大又蓝，漂亮极了。

5. Holidays

去年我和爸爸妈妈一起去了西班牙的一个小岛度假。小岛虽然小，但是海水很干净，而且非常漂亮。这里的人十分友好，但是他们只会说西班牙语，不会说英语。不过我在学校学习西班牙语，所以我可以练习西班牙语。小岛上的食物非常好吃，有很多海鲜。我和妈妈太喜欢海鲜了，但是爸爸只爱吃肉，不喜欢海鲜。小岛上的天气太热了，我被晒伤了。

6. Staying in a Hotel

我住在海边的酒店，酒店又大又干净。这里除了有游泳池以外，还有三个网球场。酒店很舒服，能看到大海，就是太贵了。

7. Holiday Plans

马田：丽丽，你今年暑假想做什么？
丽丽：我想去三亚，因为三亚的天气非常好，每天都是晴天。
马田：你想住在哪儿？
丽丽：我想住在一个酒店里。酒店有游泳池，我可以每天游泳。
马田：小明，你今年暑假想做什么？
小明：我想去西班牙，我去过西班牙，西班牙人很友好，食物也很好吃。
马田：你想在西班牙待几天？
小明：一个星期吧。
马田：珊珊，你的暑假呢？
珊珊：我要去中国旅行，我要去北京、上海、西安和广州。
马田：你怎么去旅行？
珊珊：我坐飞机去中国。在中国，我要坐火车，因为火车不仅快而且省钱。

VII. Lifestyle

1. Lifestyle

（1）疫情前我工作很忙，很晚睡觉，也没有时间运动。现在我每天运动半个小时。疫情以后，我会在家工作。

（2）疫情前我在饭店工作，没有时间和我的孩子们在一起。现在我可以每天和孩子们在花园踢足球、打乒乓球。明年我想回学校学习，然后换一个工作。

2. Healthy Lifestyle

Example：我觉得健康生活是多吃健康食物，少吃快餐。

（1）我觉得健康生活是早睡觉，早起床。

（2）我觉得健康生活是每天都要快乐，少生气。

（3）我觉得健康生活是多运动，少喝酒。

VIII. Social and Global Issues

1. Local Environment

记者：请说一说你们对附近环境的看法，好吗？

（1）河水太脏，孩子们不能去河里游泳了。

（2）路上车太多，让空气污染越来越严重了。

（3）我们附近为什么没有回收中心？

2. Volunteer Work

（1）做义工能让我学到东西，可是工作的时候又忙又累。

（2）我太忙了，做义工需要很多时间，我没有时间。

（3）很多人认为做义工好。但是只做义工就好了吗？我不同意。

（4）做义工可以认识很多来自不同地方的朋友。

IX. Education, Future Study and Employment

1. School Life

（1）虽然我的学校离我家很远，但是学校里有很多亲切的老师和友好的同学。

（2）我觉得如果学校的图书馆能有更多书，同时也更安静一点儿，就好了。

（3）我每天在学校的食堂吃午饭，又美味又健康，就是有点儿贵。

（4）我们的体育馆又大又干净，我太喜欢在那儿上体育课了。

2. School Subjects, Routine and Life Pressure

（1）我现在总是觉得特别累，因为学习压力太大了。

（2）我常常都睡不够，因为我每天早上八点就要开始上第一节课。

（3）虽然数学和做实验也很有意思，但是我最感兴趣的是能用不同语言和来自不同国家的朋友聊天儿、开玩笑。

（4）我们的老师最近病了，我和同学们都很担心她，我们打算下个星期去医院看望她。

（5）我不想给我的好朋友看我的作业，所以现在她不跟我说话了。

3. Future Careers

李娜：我将来想成为一名老师。当老师的好处是有很多假期，坏处是压力非常大。

王龙：我以后想当演员，因为有名的演员能赚很多钱，但是出名是非常难的。

4. School Life

小李：琳琳，你的学校在中国，你能说说你的学校吗？

琳琳：我的学校很大，有四千个学生、六百个老师。我们每天有八节课，早上八点开始上课，中午十二点吃午饭，下午四点半放学。

小李：你每天上八节课累吗？

琳琳：不太累，因为我们有很多休息时间。休息的时候我可以和我的朋友聊天儿，吃东西或者运动。

小李：你的学校有什么课？

琳琳：我们有数学课、语文课、英语课、

Transcript

科学课、体育课和音乐课，等等。我最喜欢科学课，我的科学老师很有意思。我将来想做一个科学家。

小李：除了你们学校的老师以外，你还喜欢你们学校的什么？

琳琳：我还喜欢我们学校的午饭。每天中午，学校有各种各样的好吃的：米饭、包子、饺子、面条、肉和青菜，等等。

XI. Listening Practice Papers

 **Paper I**

1. My Best Friend

我的朋友叫麒麟，他上十一年级。他有长长的黑色头发。

2. Holiday Destination

Example：我圣诞节的时候去了德国圣诞市场。

（1）我圣诞节去了西班牙海边。

（2）我圣诞节去了法国山区。

3. At School

（1）我喜欢我的学校，在学校我有很多朋友。

（2）我爱上音乐课，不太喜欢数学课。

（3）学校旁边就是运动中心，我常常去练习游泳。

4. Internet

（1）我有电脑，但是我常常用手机上网。

（2）我每天上45分钟网。

（3）我一般上网和朋友聊天儿。

5. Rubbish Collection Activity

下个星期一中午我们要去公园的足球场捡垃圾。昨天那儿有比赛，留下了很多垃圾。

6. Job

我是一名厨师。我喜欢我的工作，但是我的工作太累了。

7. Festivals

去年中国新年的时候，我们包了饺子，但是没去看舞狮。今年新年我希望能收到红包。

8. A Date

小军：美美，我六点去图书馆还书，我们六点半见面吧。

美美：我们在图书馆左边的公园见面吧。

小军：见面后我们去图书馆对面看电影。

9. Eating Out

Food critic 1：昨晚我去了一家意大利餐厅，吃了一个鸡肉比萨，鸡肉太咸了。

Food critic 2：昨晚我去了一家日本饭店，吃了一碗海鲜面，面都凉了。

10. The Legendary Messi

我最喜欢的足球运动员是梅西。他以前为西班牙踢球，因为他太贵了，所以从今年夏天开始，他就不再给西班牙踢球了。梅西个子不高。除了足球，他还喜欢画画。

11. Green Life

（1）从现在开始我要节约用水。

（2）每天骑自行车去上学。
（3）帮助爸爸妈妈整理可以回收的垃圾。
（4）不买太多的衣服。
（5）不浪费食物。

12. Gap Year

（1）我上11年级,还有五个月就要考试了。
（2）考试后,我想花一年时间先去全世界旅游,学习不同的文化,然后再上大学。

13. Exchange Programme

今天我看了京剧。因为我对京剧没有兴趣,所以我觉得没意思。明天我们要去学打太极拳,我比较喜欢。

14. Volunteer Work

我们医院要招义工,请大家踊跃报名。你的工作包括陪病人散步、陪孩子做游戏。你需要会开车。

 Paper II

1. Food

Friend 1：以前我喜欢吃烤鸭,现在我经常吃牛肉,以后我要多吃蔬菜。
Friend 2：前几年,我吃很多水果,但是现在我吃太多快餐了,以后我打算多吃新鲜的海鲜。

2. Weather Forecast

（1）上个星期,我去海边度假了。第一天是阴天,多云。
（2）第二天是个大晴天,没有风也没有雨。
（3）第三天下了暴雨,特别冷。
（4）第四天特别热,但是有小风。
（5）第五天有强风,风力七到八级。

3. Music

我是一个音乐爱好者,最喜欢听乡村音乐。明天我要去听一个美国乡村音乐会。

4. Future Plans

Example：我以后不想要孩子,因为要孩子很麻烦。
（1）我长大以后想当一名警察。
（2）中学毕业以后,我想去南非做义工。
（3）我现在不知道自己以后想做什么,但是我希望自己做什么都能成功。

5. Marriage/Partnerships

（1）我上个月刚结婚,但是我和我的先生最近总是因为小事不开心。
（2）我已经离婚三年了,没有孩子,我觉得自己一个人更放松、更自由。
（3）我和女朋友的感情很好,但是我们都太年轻了,所以不打算很快结婚。

6. Holidays

暑假我想去爬长城、参观故宫。但是我妹妹说她想去爬大本钟,而且还希望能在白金汉宫里见到女王。我爸爸最爱有美丽山水的地方,所以他想去桂林。

7. Celebrities

（1）这个男演员的表演特别棒,但是他不太会穿衣服,身上的颜色太多了!
（2）她穿的这条连衣裙真是又美又酷,我也想买一条一样的。
（3）他看上去帅极了,就是领带的颜色有点儿深,和他的衬衫不配。
（4）这个女演员不但头发很乱,而且穿的

衣服也不像是来参加电影节的，更像是去超市买东西穿的。

8. Home

房子不需要很大，但是一定要有书房。最好在市中心，因为那里有很多免费的公立学校，我的孩子可以去那里上学。

9. Part-time Jobs

思思：对我来说，做兼职有好处也有坏处。好处是能赚一些零花钱，坏处是让我没有时间和家人在一起。

蓝田：我认为做兼职的好处是能有一些工作经验，但是坏处是我很少有时间跟朋友见面了。

10. Environmental Protection

为了保护环境，我们要少买没用的东西，经常回收家里用过的瓶子和旧物品。不太热的时候别用空调，也不要总开冰箱。

11. Healthy Living

Student A：我觉得食堂的饭菜虽然很健康，但是有点儿贵。

Student B：肉菜总是太少，但是想吃的人总是太多.

Student C：我们为什么只能喝水，不能喝其他饮料？

12. Media

Person 1：我喜欢在脸书或微博上发我自己的照片。希望有一天我能在网上教别人怎么穿衣服。

Person 2：我认为上网很浪费时间，因为广告太多了！我更喜欢在电视上看新闻、看电影。昨天我就在家看了一部功夫电影，精彩极了！

13. Advertisement

我们是一家网络游戏公司，现在需要一名前台。她/他需要能流利地说中文和英文，待人友好，不怕脏、不怕累。每星期工作五天，周日和周一休息。

14. Social Issues

（1）最近这些年，城市人口增加了很多，但是并没有足够的房子，导致房价上涨，这让越来越多城市里的人买不起房子。

（2）在农村，虽然医院很多，但是优秀的医生不够，当地人说政府应该给在农村工作的医生更高的工资。

15. School

我想继续留在现在的学校上12年级，因为我认识所有的老师和同学，不会有那么大的交友压力。在这里，我是真正的"如鱼得水"。

16. Festivals

（1）我最喜欢这个节日，因为我能和家人一起吃美味的"团圆饭"，还能收红包，热闹极了！

（2）我最喜欢这个节日，因为我能和妹妹一起在花园里找巧克力蛋，特别好玩儿！

Paper III

1. Sports

我叫小丽，我常常去我家附近的超市买吃的，因为超市的青菜和水果很新鲜。去超市买东西的时候，我可以走路，这对我的健康也很好。

我有很多爱好，我喜欢跑步、打网球和跳舞。每星期一，我和我的弟弟一起在公园跑步，我们会跑一个小时。有时候，我在学校打网球，我打网球打得非常好。我觉得打网球不仅很健康，而且非常有意思。去年我开始学习跳舞，我跳中国舞，也跳拉丁舞。我有一个舞蹈老师，她是法国人，她跳舞跳得很好看。明年我想参加舞蹈比赛。

2. Living Area

我的新家很大，也很漂亮，有三个卧室。我的卧室比我弟弟的卧室大，我的卧室里有一张床、一张桌子、一个电脑和一个沙发。我每天在卧室里做作业。

我住的地方在市中心。这里非常干净，有很多人，也有很多商店，买东西很方便。我家旁边有一个运动中心。周末的时候，我常常和我的朋友去运动中心打篮球。我的学校离我家很近，走路十分钟。

3. My Family and My Friends

采访者：大明，你可以介绍一下你的家吗？

大　明：可以，我家有五口人：我的爸爸妈妈、一个姐姐、一个弟弟和我。以前，我们住在北京，现在住在伦敦。我现在在一个新学校上学。

采访者：你在新学校有朋友吗？

大　明：我有一个朋友，他也上十年级，今年十五岁。他是英国人，很高，也很瘦。我们常常一起打篮球，他很喜欢帮助我。

采访者：你喜欢伦敦吗？

大　明：我很喜欢伦敦。星期一到星期五，我和我的弟弟一起去学校，我的姐姐去大学。我的爸爸是一个工程师，我的妈妈是一个医生。周末的时候，我和我的家人会一起在伦敦走走看看。

4. Holidays

小山：文文，你假期去了什么地方？

文文：我去了美国。美国很大，但是人很少。

小山：你觉得这次旅行怎么样？

文文：我太累了，因为我去了三个城市，看了很多名胜古迹，不过我很喜欢美国。

小山：娜娜，你的假期怎么样？

娜娜：假期我哪儿都没去，我每天在家里学习西班牙语，因为明年我想去西班牙上大学。

小山：你喜欢学习西班牙语吗？

娜娜：我觉得很好，很有意思。

小山：大卫，你假期做了什么？

大卫：我去了山区，我在山区散步了。

小山：你觉得山区怎么样？

大卫：山区不太好，我觉得比较浪费时间。因为除了散步，我不能做别的运动。小山，你假期做什么了？

小山：我去看我的爷爷奶奶了。他们的家很有意思，我很喜欢，但是我的爷爷奶奶觉得他们住的地方不好玩儿。

5. My School

我的学校在西安，是一个很大的中学。我的学校有三个教学楼、一个大操场、一个足球场和一个篮球场。学校里有很多教室，有音乐教室、科学教室、图书馆、体育馆、礼堂和食堂，等等。我每天在食堂吃午饭。下个星期我有一个音乐表演，现在我每天都在礼堂里练习唱歌。

6. **Environmental Protection**

早上好，我们是学校的环保组织。如果你想帮助人们保护环境，请来教学楼三楼。你可以告诉人们怎么做垃圾分类、怎么节约水和电、少用塑料袋、少开车，等等。现在全球变暖的情况越来越严重，夏天发大水，冬天非常冷，我们需要保护好环境，这也需要你的帮助。在这里，你不能赚钱，但是会得到很好的工作经验。如果你想加入我们，请给我们打电话：020-33382260。

7. **Using Technology in Daily Life**

娜娜：大山，你喜欢用手机吗？
大山：我当然喜欢用手机了。我每天会用五个小时手机。
娜娜：你用手机做什么？
大山：我不仅用手机和我的朋友聊天儿、发短信，还用手机看新闻，还常常用手机听音乐。你呢？
娜娜：我不太喜欢用手机看新闻，我觉得对我的眼睛不好。我常常买杂志。我的家人也不常用手机。每天早上，我爸爸会一边喝茶一边看报纸。

8. **Traveling and Ticket Booking**

Part A

我是琳琳。上个星期我去了上海。在上海，我常常坐地铁，因为地铁不但方便，而且很便宜。我参观了博物馆，也吃了很多好吃的。我喜欢上海。

Part B

我是小明。下个星期我要去北京，我在市中心的酒店订了一个单人房。我可以走路去看名胜古迹，或者坐出租车去看长城和故宫，很方便。

Part C

我是李东。下个月我要坐飞机去澳大利亚，因为我的叔叔在澳大利亚，我可以去兼职。我爸爸给我订了单程票，我要自己赚钱买回来的飞机票。

9. **Food and Eating Out**

Part A

中国很大，有很多地方，也有很多不同的食物。比如，在南方，人们喜欢吃米饭；在北方，人们喜欢吃面条。现在，很多人用网络学习做饭，北方人可以学习南方菜，南方人可以学习北方菜，人们都可以吃上地道的菜了。上个星期，我的朋友在网上学习了一个菜，他做得非常好吃。他说做饭变得非常容易，也很有意思。

Part B

如果你觉得一个饭店的菜很好吃，你可以用抖音告诉别人，这样就会有很多人来这个饭店吃饭。他们不仅会吃饭，还会拍视频放到网上，然后这个饭店就会变得很有名。这样的饭店叫"网红饭店"。很多人都喜欢去网红饭店吃饭、打卡。

Part C

现在不仅有网红饭店，还有网红奶茶店。如果你想喝奶茶，你可以在网上找到很多网红奶茶店。网红奶茶比较贵，但是很好喝。

10. Careers

我的爸爸是一个记者,他去过很多国家。他喜欢做记者,因为可以看到很多人和他们的生活。我的妈妈在医院工作,她是一个医生,她每天都很忙。我妈妈说她的工作很重要,所以她工作很认真。我的哥哥在上大学,他学习数学和物理。他将来要做一个工程师,他觉得工程师的工作非常有意思,也很有挑战性。将来,我想做一个义工,我想去非洲国家帮助很多人。我的弟弟以后想在银行工作,因为他觉得在银行工作可以赚很多钱。